I0030640

Building on COVID-19's Innovation Momentum for Digital, Inclusive Education

Andreas Schleicher

))OECD

This work is published under the responsibility of the Secretary-General of the OECD. The opinions expressed and arguments employed herein do not necessarily reflect the official views of the Member countries of the OECD.

This document, as well as any data and map included herein, are without prejudice to the status of or sovereignty over any territory, to the delimitation of international frontiers and boundaries and to the name of any territory, city or area.

The statistical data for Israel are supplied by and under the responsibility of the relevant Israeli authorities. The use of such data by the OECD is without prejudice to the status of the Golan Heights, East Jerusalem and Israeli settlements in the West Bank under the terms of international law.

Note by Turkey
The information in this document with reference to "Cyprus" relates to the southern part of the Island. There is no single authority representing both Turkish and Greek Cypriot people on the Island. Turkey recognises the Turkish Republic of Northern Cyprus (TRNC). Until a lasting and equitable solution is found within the context of the United Nations, Turkey shall preserve its position concerning the "Cyprus issue".

Note by all the European Union Member States of the OECD and the European Union
The Republic of Cyprus is recognised by all members of the United Nations with the exception of Turkey. The information in this document relates to the area under the effective control of the Government of the Republic of Cyprus.

Please cite this publication as:
Schleicher, A. (2022), *Building on COVID-19's Innovation Momentum for Digital, Inclusive Education*, International Summit on the Teaching Profession, OECD Publishing, Paris, https://doi.org/10.1787/24202496-en.

ISBN 978-92-64-70693-4 (print)
ISBN 978-92-64-77703-3 (pdf)

International Summit on the Teaching Profession
ISSN 2312-7082 (print)
ISSN 2312-7090 (online)

FOREWORD

In May 2022, the Spanish Ministry of Education, the OECD, and Education International bring education ministers, union leaders and other teacher leaders together for the International Summit on the Teaching Profession (ISTP). Its aim is to better support the teaching profession in meeting the formidable challenges of 21st century education.

One of the secrets of the success of the International Summit on the Teaching Profession is that it explores difficult and controversial issues on the basis of internationally comparative data and analysis provided by the OECD. This report provides the background for two key themes, which the 2022 International Summit of the Teaching Profession explores.

The first session of the Summit will examine the pedagogical implications of digitalisation. This is covered in the first chapter, which is largely based on the OECD's 21st Century Children project and the OECD Digital Education Outlook, as well as the PISA and TALIS 2018 surveys.

During the pandemic, technology became a lifeline for education as schools closed down. This opened up entirely new ways for learning to become more personal and adaptive, and it gave teachers novel insight into how different students learn differently. At the same time, the COVID-19 crisis highlighted the importance of something that was not technological or digital at all: that relationships and social interactions in schools are vital for children's and young people's education. It also showed that education systems need to help schools develop their capacity and infrastructure for strong and inclusive digital learning – one that is accessible and relevant to all students and teachers. And lastly, the crisis showed us that holistic digital school strategies can better harness the potential of digital tools.

How can technology empower learners and teachers rather than disempower them? How can artificial intelligence-enabled learning that is tailored to each person help close rather than amplify learning gaps? And how do we make sure that data is protected and that technologies are ethical and transparent? This new kind of learning works best when teachers are at the centre of the design, development and implementation of digital learning environments. It works when governments and unions work together so that students and teachers are not just consumers of digital technologies but co-creators and designers of innovative learning environments. Technologically-enhanced teaching and learning works best when there is collaboration among education's many stakeholders. Working together encourages the integration of new pedagogical approaches; better compatibility between different technologies; and the shift in attention from learning technology to learning activities. These are the issues the Summit will explore in the first session.

The second session explores how more inclusive school systems can be drivers of more inclusive societies. This is covered in the second chapter, which is largely based on the OECD working paper *The social and economic rationale of inclusive education*.

The pandemic has exposed the flaws and inequities in our school systems. Often, the digital learning environment for modern education has been inadequate. Many students have suffered from the absence of supportive environments for learning, and there have been missed opportunities to unleash local initiatives and align resources with needs. However, the pandemic has also shown how schools have been creative and innovative, and teachers, parents and students worked together on new forms of learning and ways to protect health.

How can school systems, school communities, teachers and policy makers work together to design and implement education policies that will not just enhance the equity of their education systems but ensure that they contribute to more inclusive communities and societies? What can teacher unions and governments do to improve schools, including those with significant numbers of students with disabilities and/or those from socially and economically deprived backgrounds? How can we achieve equity and inclusion, and how will we know when we have? The Summit will explore these issues in the second session.

This report provides data and analysis from the OECD as background for ministers and union leaders to address these questions. It was prepared by Andreas Schleicher, based on contributions from Hannah Ulferts, Francesca Gottschalk, Pablo Fraser and Cecilia Mezzanotte. Cassandra Davis, Clara Young, Stephen Flynn and Della Shin provided support in the editorial process, as well as in production. The report is based on data, comparative analysis and reports from the OECD.

Andreas Schleicher

Director for Education and Skills and Special Advisor on Education Policy to the Secretary-General

TABLE OF CONTENTS

EXECUTIVE SUMMARY

Nothing has hit education systems across the globe harder and more thoroughly than school closures during the COVID-19 pandemic. The disruption has yielded many observations, but two are particularly important. Firstly, digitalisation has not just helped maintain teaching and learning during school closures but transformed it. Schools are now waking up to a digital world that will fundamentally change learning. Secondly, students, schools and education systems that were not ready for this transition have fallen significantly behind. Inequities in digital infrastructure and equipment, and people's digital skills are but one aspect of many education systems' insufficient inclusivity. Digitalisation and inclusive education are two of the themes of the 2022 International Summit of the Teaching Profession. This report looks at the pedagogical implications of digitalisation and how inclusive education can be the driver of more inclusive societies.

Chapter 1 discusses the effectiveness and anytime-anywhere flexibility of education technologies. To teachers, the collaborative possibilities they open up are also of growing interest. Digitalisation can boost professional learning and exchange among teachers and schools. Online education communities strengthen teachers' networks, allowing them to co-create and share best practices gained from research and classroom experience.

Perhaps the most transformative force in education, however, is artificial intelligence (AI). Though still early days, data-driven personalised learning allows students to take greater ownership over how they learn and where they learn. Technology can take over teachers' routine tasks, freeing them for what matters most: working directly with students. Real-time classroom analytics displayed on a dashboard can tell teachers what they may be missing: students who are having trouble following a lesson, who source information poorly or who are bored, for example. The report cautions, however, that integration of AI software into teaching requires well-deliberated policy on ethics, fairness, transparency, safety, accountability and data privacy.

Interactive table tops, gamification, simulations and augmented reality are the new digital tools in hands-on blended learning. But technology has evolved much faster than pedagogy so we need to help teachers leverage its potential. While COVID-19 expediencies of remote learning sped up everyone's digital uptake, this did not take place in optimal circumstances. What do we know about teachers' formal training in digital and media literacy?

According to the OECD's Teaching and Learning International Survey (TALIS) 2018, only 56% of teachers in OECD countries received formal training in digital technologies for teaching and only 43% felt it had properly prepared them. We also know that educating students about online risks was left out of most teachers' professional development.

Teachers would benefit from explicit training on online risks and, on the flip side, positive engagement in the digital sphere. This kind of digital citizenship requires tech competence and engagement; critical thinking in digital spaces; the ability to negotiate platforms and source reliable information; a readiness to interpret, understand and express oneself through digital means; and empowerment over one's data rights and right to privacy. Generally, education – especially in secondary and not earlier – focuses on students' basic operational digital skills rather than combining them with social and creative ones, including the capacity to create digital content. A more comprehensive digital skills approach would generate more positive tangible outcomes.

How should digital and media literacy be integrated into school curricula? Generally, digital skills are integrated into existing subjects or feature as independent classes or units. Some countries are entirely overhauling their curriculum or have already done so. What is key is that media and digital literacy learning be holistic. It works best when students' voices on the subject are heard and when parents, teachers, computer experts, health professionals, psychologists, law enforcement and community organisations are involved.

Unleashing digitalisation's full potential in education requires unprecedented investment in technology and professional development. Education systems must be ready to partner with the private sector. Beyond financial implications, it is a collaboration that should extend to the design process of education software to ensure that it is inclusive of minority populations of students.

Chapter 2 is devoted to inclusive education. Vulnerable students, especially, have suffered socially, emotionally and academically because of the COVID-19 crisis; they deserve special attention in its aftermath. The long-term consequences of pandemic-induced learning gaps are estimated to be an average decline of 3% in individual earnings. These students may also experience more fragile social, emotional and physical health in the future.

The report looks at equitable opportunities that even out the disadvantages of students' particular socio-economic backgrounds. Economic arguments for inclusive education encompass poverty reduction and the productivity gains obtained by improving the academic outcomes of low-performing students. On the opposite side of the balance sheet, the costs societies incur by not supporting disadvantaged students include losses in gross domestic product (GDP) and tax revenues, and rises in social welfare and health spending.

The equity gap in OECD education systems was spotted well before the pandemic. Data from TALIS 2018 show that, on average across OECD countries, at least one in five teachers (22%) needed training on special education needs (SEN), with a significant shortage of teachers able to teach students with SEN in lower secondary. Regarding immigrant and refugee students, TALIS 2018 shows that, on average, one in three teachers (33%) did not feel sufficiently equipped to teach in multicultural settings. This is critical when one considers that 17% to 30% of teachers in OECD countries work in schools with culturally or linguistically diverse student populations. From simply a numerical point of view, classrooms are insufficiently inclusive of refugee students: a refugee child is five times more likely to be excluded from school than a non-refugee.

We see the marginalisation of other diverse groups as well. The enrolment rates of Roma children in early childhood education across Europe are far below that of the population average, with higher drop-out rates later on in education. Students with an Indigenous background, gifted students and those in LGBTQI+ communities are all, in varying degrees, more vulnerable to poorer socio-emotional and academic outcomes in non-inclusive schools.

The benefits of inclusive education are manifold. Studies show that students with special educational needs do better academically in inclusive settings and are more likely to enrol in higher education. Cultures that are more gender-equal are associated with a reduction in the negative gender gap in mathematics. But the most compelling argument for inclusive compulsory education is its potential for strengthening social cohesion. In countering our natural intolerances and hidden biases, and expanding our world and belief that we can excel, education that reaches out to all students is one that cultivates trust, that most intangible of bonds holding societies together.

01
EDUCATING 21ST CENTURY CHILDREN IN THE DIGITAL WORLD

During the pandemic technology became a lifeline for education and it opened up entirely new ways for learning to become more personal and adaptive, and for teachers to obtain novel insight into how different students learn differently. At the same time, the pandemic has highlighted the importance of the social and relational value of schools in the education of children and young people. It has shown that education systems need to have a strong and inclusive digital learning infrastructure and system capacity to support schools in a way that is accessible and relevant to all students and teachers. It has also emphasised the importance of digital school strategies that integrate all relevant aspects to harness the potential of digital tools.

THE POTENTIAL OF DIGITAL TECHNOLOGIES

The OECD's Digital Education Outlook (OECD, 2021[1]) provides a multitude of examples for the use of technology in education.

- Computer tutors or intelligent tutoring systems provide students with a learning experience where the learning system adapts the presentation based on a model or ongoing assessment of the student, a model of the subject area being learned, and a model of how to teach (Wenger, 1987[2]). Each of these models can be more sophisticated or more basic. Baker (2016[3]) notes that contemporary intelligent tutoring systems tend to be sophisticated in only one area (which differs between systems) and very simple in other areas.

- Digital learning games embed learning into a fun activity that resembles a game. The degree of gamification can vary from activities that embed learning into core gameplay and which may not even seem to be a learning activity (see, for instance, SimCity and Civilisation) to more obvious learning activities where the student is rewarded for successful performance (for instance, getting to throw a banana at a monkey after answering a math problem correctly in MathBlaster).

- Simulations are computerised imitations of a process or activity that would be difficult or costly to do in the real world as an educational activity. Increasing numbers of students today use virtual laboratories to conduct experiments that could be dangerous, expensive, or difficult, and also to receive feedback and learning support while completing these activities.

- Virtual reality systems embed learners in 3D depictions of real-world activities. Like simulations, they make it feasible to engage in activities from a home or computer lab that would be expensive, dangerous, or simply impossible to engage in otherwise. Augmented reality systems embed additional information and experiences into real-world activities, ranging from pop-up details that appear and ambient displays (information that is available in the environment without having to focus on it) to overlaying a different world on top of the current one. Both augmented reality and virtual reality often rely upon headsets to present visual information to learners.

- Educational robots have a physical presence and interact with students in real-world activities to support their learning. While robots as educational DIY kits have been available since the 1980s, a recent development sees robots take up the role of tutor.

- Massive online open courses (MOOCs) provide students with a basic learning experience, typically consisting of videos and quizzes. The innovation around MOOCs is not in the learning experience – it is typically a simplified version of a large lecture class – but, rather, in making materials developed by faculty at world-famous universities, often on highly specialised topics, accessible to learners around the world.

- With new developments and diversification of digital technologies, there has been a boom in the development of artificial intelligence, which can include pattern recognition, decision making and processing language. For example, learning algorithms can detect online behavioural patterns, and then use these patterns to influence things like search results and advertising. Other ways in which artificial intelligence is prominent in the daily lives of children and adults is through virtual assistants, such as Siri (Apple) and Alexa (Amazon). Voice recognition allows children to relay various commands to these tools, and the anthropomorphic framing (i.e. giving a name and a human voice to both Siri and Alexa) can help stimulate empathy for them. There are opportunities for artificial intelligence to help education systems around the world as well. For example, the use of artificial intelligence can help promote personalised learning by taking over routine tasks thereby freeing up teachers' time to work with their students directly (Pedró et al., 2019[4]). Despite these huge opportunities, issues such as ethics, fairness, transparency, safety, accountability and privacy feature heavily in policy agendas focused on artificial intelligence (OECD, 2019[5]).

As computerised educational technologies become more commonly accessible to teachers and students, there is increasing awareness that the technology does not simply increase convenience for teachers or provide a fun alternative activity for students – it can promote new methods for teaching and learning.

PERSONALISED LEARNING

One major trend within learning, driven by these technologies, is the move towards personalising learning to a greater degree. Personalisation of learning did not start with computerised technology – in a sense, it has been available since the first use of one-on-one tutoring, thousands of years ago (if not earlier). However, with the increase in systematised, standardised schooling and teaching over a hundred years ago, awareness increased that many students' learning needs were being poorly met by one-size-fits-all curricula. Classroom approaches such as mastery learning (each student works on material until mastery and only then moves on to the next topic) were developed, but proved difficult to scale due to the demands on the teacher. Educational technologies provided a ready solution to this problem – the computer could manage some of the demands of personalising learning, identifying each individual student's degree of mastery and providing them with learning activities relevant to their current position within the curriculum.

A student's knowledge or state of learning was the first thing that educational technologies became effectively personalised for. Molenaar (2021[6]) details efforts to develop better personalisation of learning for learners, providing a framework for the degree of automation in personalised learning systems. She discusses the shift from teacher-driven systems to computer-based technologies that can take a larger role in immediate decision making, remaining within guidelines and goals specified by the teacher.

Next, educational technologies became more effective at personalising for differences in students' self-regulated learning – their ability to make good choices during learning that enhance their learning outcomes and efficiency. Modern educational technologies in many cases have the ability to recognise when students are using ineffective or inefficient strategies, and to provide them with recommendations or nudges to get back onto a more effective trajectory.

A contemporary trend, which is still primarily in research classrooms rather than wide-scale deployment, is the move towards recognising and adapting to student engagement, affect, and emotion. These systems recognise these aspects of a student's experience either from their interaction and behaviour within the system or from physical and physiological sensors. There are now several examples of educational technologies – particularly intelligent tutoring systems and games – that have been able to identify a student who is bored, frustrated, or gaming the system (trying to find strategies to complete materials without needing to learn) and re-engage them productively (DeFalco et al., 2017[7]).

Increasingly, research also looks at trying to personalise to increase broader motivation or interest. This work differs from the work on engagement and affect in terms of time-scale. Whereas engagement and affect often manifest in brief time periods – as short as a few seconds – motivation and interest are more long-term stable aspects of student experience. Work by Kizilcec and colleagues (Kizilcec et al., 2017[8]), for instance, has tried to connect student learning experiences with their values, leading to greater degrees of completion of online courses. Elsewhere, the contents of learning systems have been modified to match student personal interests, leading students to work faster, become disengaged less often, and learn more.

NEW PEDAGOGIES

Although the most obvious impact of artificially intelligent educational technologies is through personalising learning directly, new pedagogies and teacher practices have also emerged. These pedagogies and practices enable teachers to support their students or provide them with experiences in ways that were generally not feasible prior to the technology's advent.

Perhaps the largest shift has been in the information available to teachers. Dashboards provide teachers with data on a range of aspects of their students' performance and learning. This has produced a major shift in how homework is used. In the past, homework would need to be brought to class by students. It could be graded by the teacher after that (meaning that feedback and learning support would be delayed), or students could grade it with the teacher in a large group, which is not a very time-efficient approach. In contrast, data from homework technologies today can become available to teachers in real time. This means that teachers can identify which students are struggling and which materials students struggled on in general before class even starts. This enables strategies where, for instance, teachers identify which students displayed common errors and can identify students who can demonstrate both incorrect and correct problem-solving strategies for whole-class discussion. It also enables teachers to message students who are behind in completing materials (or even in starting to work through materials), helping get the student back on track (Arnold and Pistilli, 2012[9]).

Similar uses are available for formative assessment systems, which are being increasingly used in contexts where students have high-stakes end-of-year examinations. These systems often go beyond teacher-designed homework in terms of their breadth and comprehensiveness of coverage of key skills and concepts. They are increasingly used by teachers to determine what topics to review with their classes as well as what types of supplemental supports to provide to specific students.

There is also better information available to teachers on what is going on in their classes in real time. Classroom analytics can provide the teacher with information on a range of aspects of class performance, from individual students' difficulties with material in real time to the relative effectiveness of collaboration by different student groups. A teacher cannot watch every student (or every student group) at all times – better data can help them understand where to focus their efforts, and which students would benefit from a conversation right now.

Beyond just providing better data, it is possible to use technology to give students a range of experiences that were not feasible a generation ago. There is new potential in having robots interact with students in classrooms.

Using simulations and games in class can enable teachers to demonstrate complex and hard-to-understand systems to students. They can also allow students to explore and interact with these systems on their own. There seems to be particular educational benefit to the combination of a rich simulation or game experience that enables a student to develop informal, practical understanding, and then a teacher lecture or explanation that helps a student bridge from that informal understanding to more formal, academic conceptual understanding (Asbell-Clarke et al., 2020[10]). Modern technologies also offer new potential for collaborative learning with systems like interactive tabletops that can scaffold effective collaboration strategies and provide rich experiences around which to collaborate.

DEVELOPING DIGITAL CITIZENSHIP

In education systems around the world, an increasing emphasis has been placed on digital citizenship. Interest in academic and policy spheres has resulted in a number of different definitions, but in a broad sense, digital citizenship can be conceptualised as norms of behaviour regarding the use of digital technologies (Ribble, Bailey and Ross, 2004[11]). It requires both educational and technological competence, as well as access to technology.

In addition, digital citizens possess the competences to actively, responsibly and positively engage in online and offline communities. Some scholars argue for inclusion of online civic engagement in the digital literacy definition alongside respectful and tolerant behaviour towards others (UNICEF, 2017[12]).

In 2018 and 2019, the OECD carried out its 21st Century Children Policy Questionnaire, which explored issues of new technologies, emotional well-being, families and peers, and physical health for children in the 21st century. Regarding digital citizenship, 13 education systems out of the 24 that responded to this section identified it as a pressing challenge in their context. This online challenge was often mentioned as having offline implications – responses highlighted that digital citizenship can contribute positively to personal development and to society as a whole, and that this can be developed in tandem with skills/knowledge pertaining to moral and civic education more generally.

The main themes that emerged from this section of the Policy Questionnaire were:

- the need to be responsible and respectful online
- the importance of offline implications (i.e. negative or maladaptive behaviours in online spaces can affect offline behaviour patterns as well)
- safety concerns – recognising harmful/threatening behaviour, exposure to non-ethical Internet usage
- media literacy

This section looks at policies and practices to strengthen and build digital citizenship, as well as some of the risks and conduct issues that arise with Internet use. These include cyberbullying, revenge porn and sexting, and security and protection of data. The section ends with a look at the role of parents.

Policies and practices for building digital citizenship

Digital citizenship encompasses different facets. Firstly, it requires competent and positive engagement with digital technologies, thereby allowing children to create content, socialise, use digital tools to play, communicate and learn, and to work and share. It also requires active and responsible participation, and the continuous defending of human dignity. This entails lifelong learning in formal, non-formal and informal contexts (Council of Europe, 2019[13]).

A set of essential digital skills are required to access digital resources and platforms. Students also need to understand how to apply critical thinking in digital spaces and being able to interpret, understand and express oneself through digital means. Countries use curricular reform, development of independent bodies and teacher training programmes to develop and strengthen the digital citizenship of their students. Table 1.1 below outlines some of the approaches countries have taken to build digital citizenship.

Table 1.1 Educational goals and criteria for success in ISTP jurisdictions

Approaches	Details	Examples
Curriculum	• Incorporation of digital and media literacy in the curriculum, either as an independent unit or class, incorporated into existing classes (i.e. language, mathematics, etc.) or a combination of both.	• Media and information education in **France** (2016); Teaching of ICT and informatics in the **Greek** curriculum; Media literacy and internet security included in content areas across curriculum in **Latvia** (2020); Values and principles established in the core curriculum in **Norway**, with new subject specific curriculum in 2020.
Teacher training	• Teachers in many contexts are trained in digital literacy, and how to foster digital literacy and citizenship in their students. Training is often supported or offered by different groups, through multi-group partnerships.	• Media coach training for teachers and educators in the **Flemish Community of Belgium** involving nine training sessions, an online course, and an "internship project" where participants conduct a project in their working environment.
Independent bodies, online platforms and information campaigns	• Some systems have established groups or bodies that target children's safe and responsible use of digital media. Campaigns tend to target teachers and parents, providing information or online resources to enhance digital skills, online knowledge and digital citizenship. These can involve partnerships.	• The Media Council for Children and Young People in **Denmark** informs and advises on children's use of digital media (e.g. provides movie ratings, informational articles for parents and educators); The *Jeunes et Medias* platform established in **Switzerland** with information on topics ranging from "fake news" to "happy slapping" and safety and data protection; "Superheroes on the Internet" in **Latvia**.
Partnerships	• Some partnerships are established to disseminate or develop informational tools or resources, while others are developed between interest groups and education systems to share knowledge and best practices, or help with implementation of digital citizenship programmes.	• Media coach training in the **Flemish Community of Belgium** is implemented by *Mediawijs* in collaboration with other groups, including funding from The Ministries for Media and for Education and Training as well as the European Commission.

Source: 21st Century Children Policy Questionnaire, see Burns, T. and F. Gottschalk (eds.) (2019), *Educating 21st Century Children: Emotional Well-being in the Digital Age,* Educational Research and Innovation, OECD Publishing, Paris, available at https://doi.org/10.1787/b7f33425-en (accessed on 1 April 2022).

A number of education systems have embedded the teaching of digital skills, as well as information and media literacy programmes, in their strategies to target digital citizenship. These approaches either involve development of a new curriculum, or integration of digital media and skills training into the existing curriculum, either as an independent unit of study or through already existing courses, or a mix of both approaches. Some systems address digital citizenship education more explicitly, such as in Saskatchewan (Canada) with *Digital Citizenship Education in Saskatchewan Schools*, which spans kindergarten to Grade 12 (the last year of high school).

Approaches targeting digital citizenship are most effective if they include a component that works to build the digital skills of teachers themselves. However, explicit training in many of these areas is not always widely available to teachers, as shown in Figure 1.1.

While over half of the 24 systems that responded to this question in the Policy Questionnaire reported that educating students in digital citizenship and digital literacy was either required or widely available, an almost equal number reported that these topics were only covered in some programmes or not widely available. Even more strikingly, despite the policy attention paid to cyber risks, educating students about online risks was the least commonly required element included in initial and continuing professional development of teachers. These findings align with the results from the Teaching and Learning International Survey (TALIS), in which teachers have consistently reported a high need for professional development in the use of ICT for teaching over the last 10 years (OECD, 2019[14]).

Figure 1.1 **Digital skills in teacher education (initial and continuous)**

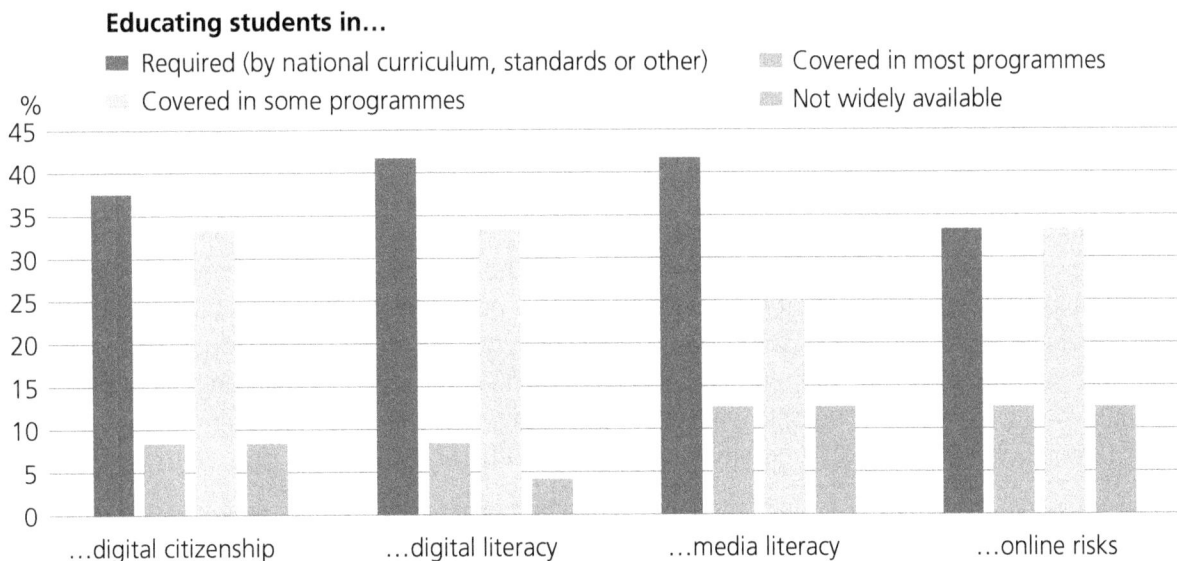

Educating students in...
- Required (by national curriculum, standards or other)
- Covered in most programmes
- Covered in some programmes
- Not widely available

Note: Responses indicate the proportion of systems that confirmed the topics were covered in existing teacher education in their systems. 24 countries and systems responded to this question.
Source: 21st Century Children Policy Questionnaire, see Burns, T. and F. Gottschalk (eds.) (2019), *Educating 21st Century Children: Emotional Well-being in the Digital Age*, Educational Research and Innovation, OECD Publishing, Paris, available at https://doi.org/10.1787/b7f33425-en (accessed on 1 April 2022).

The role of parents

The most effective strategies for promoting digital citizenship are those that involve a multi-stakeholder, multi-sectoral approach, including engagement from parents and children themselves. However, empowering parents to guide their children online requires them to have the necessary digital skills to do this effectively. This is challenging on two levels. First, research has demonstrated that on average, parents tend to have higher digital literacy skills than their children until they reach around 12 years of age. After a short period of similar skill level, children, on average, surpass their parents by the age of 15. This results in parents not necessarily being able to guide their older children in their online experiences (Byrne et al., 2016[15]).

Second, not all children are able to turn to their parents. Children from disadvantaged homes are more likely to have parents with lower digital skills, and those parents are less likely to be involved in their schooling. Conflicts with work schedules, childcare needs, transportation problems, lack of familiarity with the institution and not speaking the same language as the teacher are just some of the participation barriers faced by parents (OECD, 2017[16]). This makes the involvement of schools and the broader community even more important for building digital citizenship and digital skills more generally.

One interesting example of an initiative involving both the broader community and technology experts comes from Google. 'Creators for Change' is a global programme consisting of 50 ambassadors with the responsibility of reaching adolescents aged 13-15 years old and educating them about digital citizenship. Google also seeks to reach children coming from disadvantaged backgrounds by creating a curriculum similar to the 'Creators for Change' programme and partnering with other businesses and organisations that seek to enhance the digital skills of disadvantaged youth. Recognising that poor digital literacy skills of parents can have a negative effect on child digital literacy, the programme pays particular attention to parental engagement.

EMBEDDING DIGITAL SKILLS IN THE CURRICULUM

Risk and resilience

Children need to explore and encounter different online risks in order to develop digital skills and resilience. In a psychological sense, resilience refers to the interplay of different factors (i.e. social, relationship and dispositional) that help promote positive adjustment when facing adversity. In other words, despite facing risky situations or having negative experiences, some individuals end up having relatively good outcomes (Rutter, 2007[17]). Digital resilience thus refers to children having the ability to adjust positively when facing online adversity: children need to be exposed to risk in order to build digital resilience (UNICEF, 2017[12]; Livingstone et al., 2011[18]).

Families can play an important role in mediating children's experiences online. Enabling and restrictive mediation are two broad strategies.

Including digital skills in the curriculum

Schools have a role to play as well. Effective ways for schools to promote resilience include training teachers in digital risks and implications; fostering a zero-tolerance approach to behaviours such as cyberbullying; and incorporating ethics and e-safety learning opportunities in the curriculum (OECD, 2018[19]).

Teachers need to recognise their importance in supporting young people in their uses of technology. Young people are not all experts, and just like all areas of education, adults have a responsibility to support young people in their endeavours. Stakeholders need to decide whether to continue down the current path and see the same patterns of behaviour or more actively intervene in providing support for young people of all ages in their uses of technology.

This relates to wider questions of the role of schooling in society. Schools have three inter-related functions: to enable young people to acquire qualifications that reflect their "knowledge skills and dispositions to be able to do something"; to facilitate (in both unintended and intended ways) the ways that young people "become part of particular social, cultural, and political 'orders' (i.e., socialisation)"; and help young people "to become more autonomous and independent in their thinking and acting" (i.e. subjectification) (Biesta, 2015[20]). Most of the focus on young people and technology use in schools is accomplished through the prism of qualifications and skills, ignoring subjectification and socialisation. However, such important aspects of schooling should not be ignored in relation to technology.

One way to achieve all three roles of schooling is to incorporate a critical digital literacies agenda into schools, enabling young people to challenge the status quo regarding technology, learning and everyday life, and to support a more holistic transition to adulthood. Such a move would be in contrast to the relatively narrow digital skills agenda in many countries that focus on the need for young people to code. Indeed, there has been much analysis and debate about the need for a more democratic educational agenda related to digital skills policies. Many people are concerned that there is a significant disconnect between what young people want and need to learn as part of their formal education and what schools offer. This could be achieved in many ways. For example, there is increasing support for 'critical digital design' that brings together the production of artefacts with a focus on ethics (i.e. drawing attention to the power relations and inequalities that are apparent in current society). There is also an emphasis on the personal (i.e., the way individuals make meaning when engaging with technology in everyday life can be understood as a learning resource), and supporting students' agency and identity development (Pangrazio, 2014[21]).

Similarly, there are important issues to explore in relation to who is setting the technology agenda, and how the current landscape is dominated by a few commercial actors. There are many implications of this, but one significant set of questions is around young people's data rights and right to privacy. This is an issue both in and outside schools and is particularly important for policy makers. Indeed, education is distinct from other domains in which big data are being applied, and needs special consideration, particularly for younger age groups. There needs to be a more holistic view of how and where learning and education takes place, and by whom, to ensure that all institutions engaged in learning (not just formal educational institutions) are accountable; and that the rights, needs and experiences of all young people are recognised.

Education systems take different approaches to teaching and learning digital skills in their curricula. Figure 1.2 highlights how different skills are incorporated into teaching and learning either as an independent subject, incorporated into existing course content or through a combination of the two. Generally, digital skills are integrated into existing subjects or are integrated and feature as independent classes or units. Some countries are engaging, or have already engaged, in an overhaul of the curriculum, whereas others are incorporating digital skills across the existing curriculum. Having a sound grasp on operational, critical thinking and social skills in digital spaces will allow for children to effectively harness the available resources to gain insight into their own health and well-being.

Figure 1.2 **How systems incorporate digital skills into teaching and learning**

■ Independent class or unit   ■ Integrated into existing subjects   ■ Both

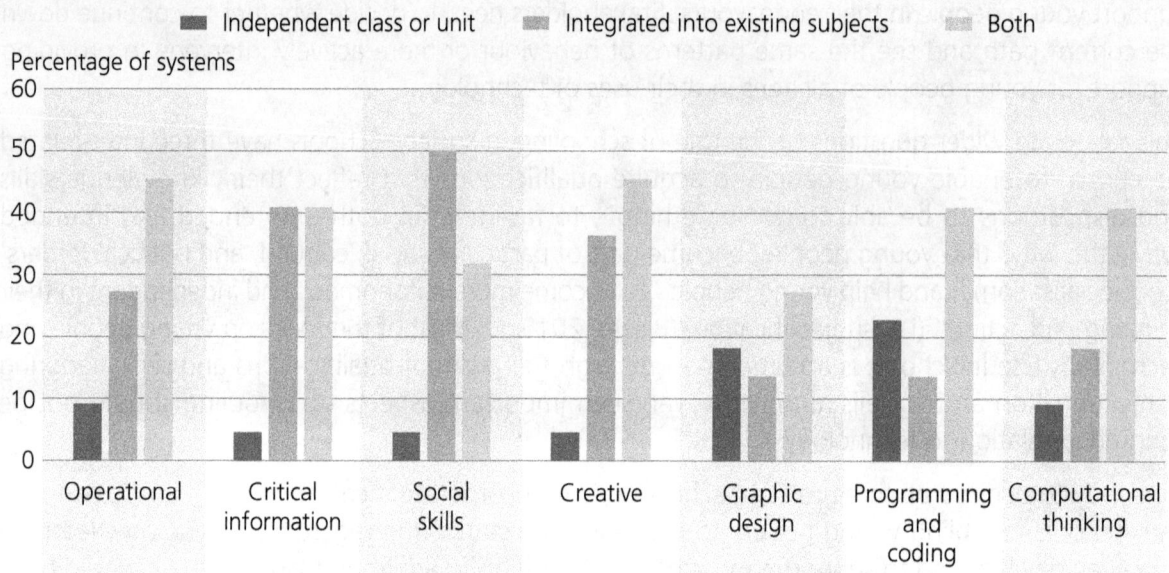

Note: Respondents were asked which digital skills were taught in school, and how these were taught. 22 countries and systems responded to this question.
Source: Burns, T. and F. Gottschalk (eds.) (2020), *Education in the Digital Age: Healthy and Happy Children, Educational Research and Innovation*, OECD Publishing, Paris, https://doi.org/10.1787/1209166a-en (accessed 01 April 2022).

To highlight one example, the Danish Ministry of Education launched a three-year experiment in compulsory education. Running from 2018-2021, with DKK 68 million of funding, it examined the importance of technology and automation in society, with a focus on ethics, security and consequences of digital technologies. Some of the digital skills it focuses on include: computational thinking/informatics, knowledge of networks and algorithms, programming, abstraction, pattern recognition and data modelling.

OECD's 21st Century Children Policy Questionnaire also queried at which level of education various digital skills are taught (see Figure 1.3).

Most systems explicitly teach operational, critical informational, social and creative skills in primary and secondary school. There is less of a focus at all levels of education on graphic design, programming/coding and computational thinking, and generally there is more of a focus on digital skills in general in secondary than in primary education or earlier. Approaches targeting digital skills often overemphasise the role of basic operational skills despite the indication that combining skills such as social and creative skills, and the capacity to create digital content can generate positive tangible outcomes (Helsper, Van Deursen and Eynon, 2015[22]). It is therefore encouraging to note the emphasis on critical information, social and creative skills in many systems alongside basic operational skills.

Figure 1.3 **Learning digital skills at different levels of education**

Systems were asked if the following skills were taught, and if so at which level of education

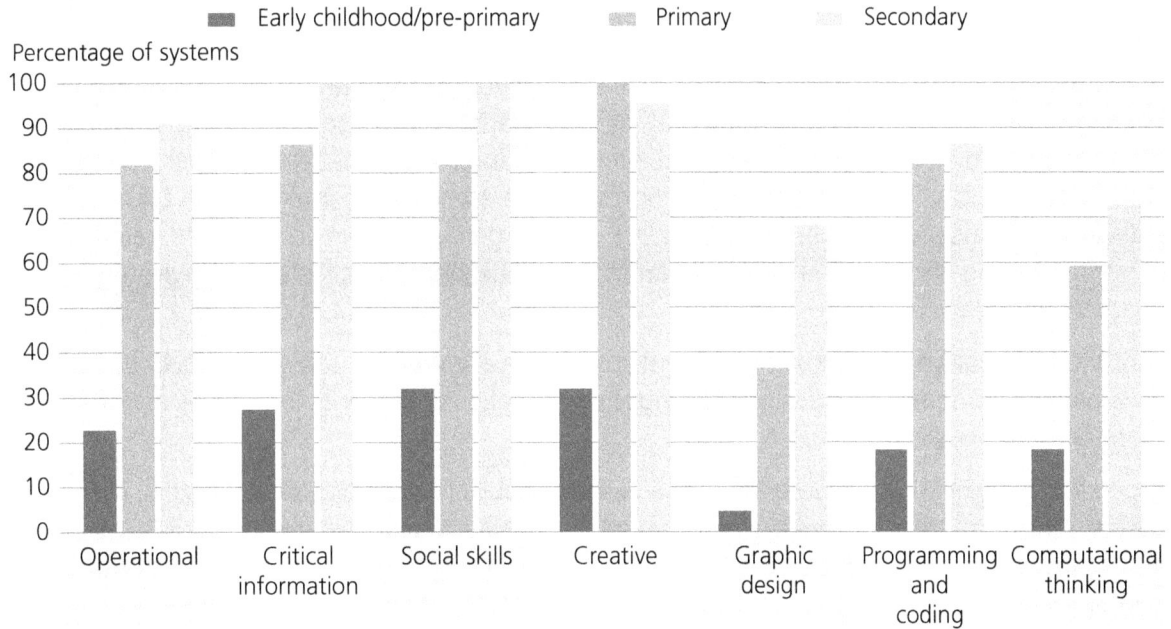

Note: 22 systems responded to this part of the Policy Questionnaire.
Source: 21st Century Children Policy Questionnaire, see Burns, T. and F. Gottschalk (eds.) (2019), *Educating 21st Century Children: Emotional Well-being in the Digital Age*, Educational Research and Innovation, OECD Publishing, Paris, available at https://doi.org/10.1787/b7f33425-en (accessed on 1 April 2022).

Designing innovative learning environments

Blended learning rethinks established routines to get more from teaching. This pedagogical approach blends student work and teaching for understanding, adapts their sequencing and draws heavily on digital learning resources. The aim is to be both more engaging and coherent for learners and to free teachers from routine practice in favour of interactive and intensive classroom activities. There are three main forms within this cluster of pedagogies:

- The inverted/flipped classroom, in which students work on material first and only then access the teacher(s) to practice, clarify and deepen understanding.

- The lab-based model in which a group of students rotates between a school lab and the classroom with the application of content through face-to-face interactions with teachers.

- 'In-Class' blending, in which individual students follow a customised schedule rotating between online and face-to-face instruction.

To be successful, blended learning calls for a profound rethinking of teacher and student roles and the willingness to adapt teaching, requiring innovation and professional engagement. When it relies on digital resources, it assumes teachers have the skill to operate technologies and an understanding of content, technology, and pedagogy in interaction. Blended learning can also be demanding of pedagogical (including digital) infrastructure and software design.

One particularly interactive aspect of blending learning involves gamification. Gamification builds on how games can capture student interest and facilitate learning. Play occupies an important place in children's learning, and supports intellectual, emotional and social well-being. It opens up potential learning experiences, driven by self-motivation and interest. Gaming in education takes different forms (e.g. gamification, game-based learning, serious games), but in this report "gamification" encompasses the pedagogical core of gaming and the benefits of playful environments for engagement and well-being.

There are two main pedagogical components: mechanical elements (rapid feedback, badges and goals, participation, and progressive challenge) and emotional elements (narratives and identities, collaboration and competition).

Gamification has been used successfully in a range of subjects, such as science, maths, languages, physical education, history, and art and design. Gamification can foster self-regulated learning, collaboration, exploration and creativity. It can also teach complex rules to players, introduce them to unfamiliar worlds, and engage them in unfamiliar tasks and logics. How to exploit the pedagogic structure of games while maintaining the element of play is a key challenge.

Computational thinking is another aspect of blended learning. It develops problem solving through computer science and looks at problems in the ways that computers do in order to solve those problems. Its techniques include approximate solutions, parallel processing, model checking, debugging, and search strategies. Its basic elements are:

- **Logical reasoning**: analyse and deduce outcomes

- **Decomposition**: break down a complex problem into smaller ones

- **Algorithms**: describe routines and create step-by-step instructions

- **Abstraction**: capture the essence of a problem, removing unnecessary detail

- **Patterns**: identify common solutions to common problems

Instead of emphasising the improvement of generic information and communication technology (ICT) skills, computational thinking takes programming and coding as a new form of literacy and as a new approach to ICTs. With computers and computer science providing interfaces between student experiences of the world and their abstract knowledge and skills, computational thinking becomes a comprehensive scientific approach and 21st century competence. It brings together a language (coding), process (problem-solving), tools (programmes), and uses experimentation and learning by doing to produce discrete outputs. Inquiry skills are developed through logical reasoning, algorithm framing and decomposition, while programming and coding foster writing abilities.

Using the international comparative International Association for the Evaluation of Educational Achievement's (IEA) Second Information Technology in Education Study Module 2 (SITES-M2) study, Law, Yuen and Fox (2011[23]) identified six dimensions of innovativeness; of those, the roles of teachers and students in learning were the most highly correlated with the innovativeness – the non-traditional nature – of the learning outcomes achieved. Further, the pedagogical innovativeness of the case studies had no correlation with the sophistication of the learning technologies adopted. In fact, Law et al. found that the innovations implemented at larger scale tend to have less ambitious educational goals as a common strategic basis for participation, requiring lower levels of innovativeness in the pedagogical practices (Law, Kampylis and Punie, 2013[24]).

Digital technologies and inclusion

With the rise in digital technologies and the convergence of digital and physical spaces, acquiring digital skills is necessary for children in the 21st century. Despite the ever-present nature of digital risks, digital tools provide near endless opportunities, for example, access to unprecedented amounts of information and opportunities for personalised learning and instruction. They enable children to create content and creatively express themselves. Indeed, research suggests that many young people turn to the Internet for health-related resources, and information seeking is a common health-related Internet use (Park and Kwon, 2018[28]). Children who are digitally skilled and media-literate will be able to search for information and resources regarding their own physical and emotional well-being. Greater media literacy will allow them to discern between information that could be misleading or fake, and promote their consumption of higher-quality information from trusted sources.

New educational technologies are typically designed with the goal of improving student and teacher experiences and outcomes. By making learning more adaptive and personal, they can enhance equity in education. However, the designers of these systems do not always consider how the full spectrum of learners are impacted. Often, systems are designed by members of specific demographic groups (typically higher socio-economic status, not identified as having special needs, and members of racial/ethnic/national majority groups) with members of their own groups in mind (not always intentionally). This can lead to lower educational effectiveness for members of other groups.

For example, Judith Good (2021[25]) discusses how there has been little effort to create educational technologies specifically designed for students with disabilities or special needs. She discusses examples of technologies that could support learners with autism, dysgraphia and visual impairment. The lack of attention to individuals with special needs by the scientific community and by developers of artificially intelligent educational technologies is a major source of inequity and a missed opportunity. Designing policies that facilitate developing systems to support learners with special needs (for instance, by developing approaches that improve access to data on disabilities while protecting student privacy) and the creation of incentives to develop for special-needs populations may help to address this inequity.

Another key area of inequity is in support of historically underserved and under-represented populations, including ethnic/racial minorities and linguistic minorities. Most educational technologies are developed by members of historically well-supported populations. They are often first piloted with members of historically well-supported populations. Testing for effectiveness with historically under-represented populations often occurs only in later stages of development (or in final large-scale evaluations of efficacy) when it is too late to make major design changes. There is increasing evidence that both educational research design findings and algorithms obtained on majority populations can fail to apply or function more poorly for other populations of learners (Ocumpaugh et al., 2014[26]; Karumbaiah, Ocumpaugh and Baker, 2019[27]).

Box 1.1 Get (media) smart

Being media literate is important in the 21st century. Children need the skills to discern fact from fiction, to determine the quality of information they consume, and to be able to find trustworthy sources online especially when it comes to their health and well-being. Alongside media literacy, developing a baseline level of science literacy so that individuals can understand how knowledge is produced and how to interpret scientific findings is important. In general, more highly educated people are more confident in science as they are able to leverage their skills in understanding it. Together, science and the media are important influencers of civic values and discourse. Learning to be discerning consumers of both will help children now and in the future to make good decisions surrounding their health, well-being, and more generally in other areas of their civic, educational and social lives.

Developing media literacy is something that many education systems around the OECD are investing in and focusing on through expanding curricula, implementing school-based programmes and fostering partnerships with key actors working in the media literacy space (OECD, 2019[29]). Programmes can target media literacy and promote individuals to engage in health information sharing. Some examples developed by Canadian non-profit organisation MediaSmarts include:

- Break the Fake: teaches four main skills for developing habits in finding and verifying information online, understanding that it is imperative to verify information before sharing it.

- Check then Share: aimed at information around COVID-19, providing concrete tools such as a dedicated search engine to find information from trusted expert sources. It promotes sharing of reliable information to improve the ratio of quality to weak or misinformation.

Other media literacy interventions take a gamified approach, tapping into children's habits and tendencies to play online games, and are therefore able to rather seamlessly integrate into their daily lives. One example of this is the Bad News Game where players become fake news tycoons, gaining followers by spreading disinformation. Games of this nature can help people (as these are not limited to children) in preparing themselves on how to encounter and combat misinformation or conspiracy theories which they may come across online. There are a plethora of online resources that can be used to promote media literacy in children. Forming key partnerships with well-trusted experts and organisations working on these initiatives should be high on education policy agendas.

Box 1.2 **Digital divides for teachers**

Education systems take a number of approaches to provide access to digital technologies. However, access to software or hardware does not directly translate into good pedagogical practice, and access to these tools does not necessarily ensure integration into classroom activities. To effectively implement them as a learning device in the classroom, teachers require technological knowledge and digital competence, as well as pedagogical and content knowledge. When teachers are able to effectively integrate technologies into their practice, it can add value to traditional instruction. Teachers who are confident and who possess the necessary skills can employ practices such as blended learning, which can help them improve differentiation of instruction according to student needs and foster classroom interaction (Paniagua and Istance, 2018[30]).

Some pre-service teachers have limited experiences learning with ICT in their training and, in some instances, the training they receive is of poor quality. According to TALIS 2018, only 56% of teachers in OECD countries received training in the use of ICT for teaching as part of their formal education or training, and only 43% felt well- or very well-prepared for this when they had completed their initial teacher education (OECD, 2019[14]). As was the case in TALIS 2013, teachers still report a high level of need for professional development in ICT skills for teaching, second only to teaching students with special needs (OECD, 2019[14]; OECD, 2014[31]). It is essential for teachers to receive quality training in the use of digital tools to integrate ICTs effectively into their practice. Teachers who are confident in their ICT abilities and who recognise the added value of ICT for teaching and learning report higher levels of ICT use during lessons, and professional development has been linked to teacher confidence (Valtonen et al., 2015[32]).

Responses to the 21st Century Children Policy Questionnaire highlight that in the majority of systems, teachers receive training in digital skills (i.e. their abilities to use digital technologies) and in the use of technology in teaching. However, teachers are not necessarily trained in a number of other important digital competencies such as assessing online risks to students and in educating students in digital literacy or digital citizenship. Teacher education at both the initial preparation and continuing professional development levels will have to expand to better prepare and support teachers to teach these important 21st century skills.

The 21st century saw a shift in importance from physical access to digital technologies, and to digital skills and usage (Van Dijk, 2017[33]) with the emergence of the notion of the second digital divide (Hargittai, 2002[34]). Research suggests that despite their reputation as so-called "digital natives", 21st century children still face inequalities in access, motivations, usage and skills regarding the Internet (Mascheroni and Ólafsson, 2016[35]). As with the first digital divide, demographic factors influence motivations for using the Internet. But some findings suggest that it is not so much who people and what their backgrounds are that matter when it comes to inequalities in outcomes of Internet use as it is what they do online and the state of their digital skills (Van Deursen and Helsper, 2018[36]).

Countries take different approaches to targeting this second digital divide. Many approaches focus on different factors associated with the promotion of digital skills and inclusion; these can be part of broader strategies targeting lifelong learning. They can also encompass higher education as well as compulsory education. For example, in Ireland (ICT Skills Action Plan) and Portugal (InCoDe.2030), wide-ranging policies with different pillars and targets are implemented to address the second digital divide. In contrast, in Australia, more targeted policies tackle different elements such as teacher education and curriculum development. Generally, policy and action plans target curriculum or support for curriculum implementation, learning frameworks, teacher education, extracurricular activities, and providing information to stakeholders on how to target digital skills and inclusion of children.

Tackling the second digital divide is a priority in many systems given the increasing emphasis on digital methods to deliver lessons and test students, and for student studying. This has been significantly amplified during the pandemic. In many countries, national tests have been digitalised. Systems such as Korea's are also integrating digital textbooks into their classrooms.

SUPPORTING TEACHERS

Educating teachers for the challenges of modern classrooms is a complex and multifaceted endeavour. Breaking patterns and learning new behaviours requires ongoing training and preparation as well as support and capacity building (OECD, 2010[37]). But education systems are not always particularly successful on this front: TALIS 2018 reveals that although many teachers actively participate in professional development, they consistently report urgent needs in teaching students with special needs and using ICT skills for teaching. The most commonly cited reasons for not taking part in available training were "conflict with work schedule" (54%) and "no incentives for participating in professional development" (48%) (OECD, 2019[14]).

Countries generally provide support to teachers to acquire digital skills and to use technology in their teaching. Some 15 of the 24 countries responding to this question in the Policy Questionnaire that digital skills and ability to use technology were required (by national curriculum, standards or other) and another five indicated that it was covered in most programmes. Similarly, 16 of the 24 countries indicated that skills in using technology in teaching were required (by national curriculum, standards or other) and another two indicated that it was covered in most programmes.

Table 1.2 Tackling the second-level digital divide

Examples of policies and practices to tackle the second digital divide

Target	Examples
Curriculum & implementation	• **Digital Technologies in Focus (Australia):** this programme provides support for disadvantaged schools in implementing the Australian Curriculum: Digital Technologies through specialist digital technologies and provision of ICT Curriculum Officers. • **Digital Literacy School Grants (Australia):** this initiative funds projects in schools supporting innovative ways of implementing the curriculum. Priority is given to under-represented and disadvantaged groups. • **Digital Technologies Hub (Australia):** provision of learning resources and activities to help support implementation of the curriculum. • **2020 Curriculum (Norway):** the curriculum in Norway for 2020 includes digital skills. • **ICT Skills Action Plan (Ireland):** Ireland has implemented three Skills Action Plan reforms, the most recent of which was implemented in 2019. The 2014-2018 Action Plan included provisions for promoting career opportunities to primary and secondary level students, involved curricular reform, and provision of ICT-related professional development opportunities for teachers. • **InCoDe.2030 (Portugal):** ICT has been expanded in the basic curriculum, first in a pilot of 223 schools. This was then integrated into curricular matrices of all the years of basic education across all schools. • **Saskatchewan's Practical and Applied Arts curricula (Saskatchewan, Canada):** this redesigned curriculum for k-12 includes robotics, automation and computer science.
Learning framework & school-based strategies	• **Digital Learning Framework for Schools (Ireland):** rolled out in the 2018/2019 school year, this was one component of the Digital Strategy for Schools 2015-2020. Schools and teachers are given a structure allowing them to identify where they are in terms of embedding digital technologies into teaching and learning, and how they can progress in this domain. • **National Reference Framework (Luxembourg):** the national reference framework was due for implementation in 2019. • **"Pact of Excellence" (French Community of Belgium):** each school will devise a strategy for integrating digital schools into learning and the governance of the school, with the aim of closing the digital divide. • **Digital Action Plan for Education and Higher Education (Quebec, Canada):** this action plan supports and guides the integration of new technologies in schools. It aims to achieve effective and optimal integration and use of digital technologies to promote lifelong skills development and maintenance. • **Digital Education Strategy (Czech Republic):** this initiative, proposed for 2020, aimed to ensure non-discriminatory access to digital educational resources, ensure conditions for development of digital skills in students and teachers, ensure the reinforcement of educational infrastructure, and to encourage the integration and understanding of digital technologies into schools. • **National Strategy for the digitalisation of the Swedish school system 2017-2022:** digital competence is one of the three main pillars of this national strategy, alongside equity in access and usage of digital tools, and research and evaluation on the effects of digitalisation in school.

Source: 21st Century Children Policy Questionnaire, see Burns, T. and F. Gottschalk (eds.) (2019), *Educating 21st Century Children: Emotional Well-being in the Digital Age*, Educational Research and Innovation, OECD Publishing, Paris, available at https://doi.org/10.1787/b7f33425-en (accessed on 1 April 2022).

However, there was far less training available for assessing online risks or identifying signs of digital dependency in students. In the Policy Questionnaire, 30% of systems reported that training on assessment of online risks was covered only in some programmes or not at all. For identifying signs of digital dependency, 45% of systems reported that it was only covered in some programmes or not at all. These figures are at odds with the high policy priority given to online risks.

Countries appear to prioritise fostering the digital skills of teachers broadly, perhaps assuming or inferring that this will also improve their ability to assess online risks or other threats to well-being. However it is important to flag that these are unique skills and explicit attention should also be given to fostering them in teachers. This is particularly important given how quickly the landscape of online risks changes. There is also room for improvement in the training and education available to teachers in teaching these skills to their students: almost half of the systems reported that their existing teacher education programmes do not provide widespread training to teachers to educate students about online risks.

The gap between training teachers in digital skills and using technology in their teaching, and identifying online risks is important to underline. Similarly, the disconnect between educating students to develop responsible online behaviour and managing the risks of digital technologies illustrates the challenge of integrating technology in schools. One important issue is that preparing students to live in a digital(ised) society involves interdisciplinary skills and student behaviour both inside and outside of school. This makes establishing clear and coherent standards for practice much more difficult.

There are three main approaches in initial and ongoing teacher education:

- curriculum reforms and extension
- formal teacher education and training
- network approaches to teaching and learning

Curriculum reform and extension

In the Policy Questionnaire, policy makers often referred to a new national curriculum as a key resource for improving the use of technology in the classroom and fostering the teaching of digital skills. The Curriculum for Excellence in Scotland (United Kingdom) and the National Core Curriculum for Basic Education are good examples of this. In other cases, emphasis is placed on the way the curriculum provides models of how to use technology in the classroom or what should be the ideal conditions for students to develop skills critical in that area, as in the new Basic Education Curriculum in Mexico.

Countries also described measures that help teachers and schools develop certain areas of the curriculum, with a particular focus on technology. For example, Quebec (Canada), Mexico and New Zealand have developed plans to implement digital technologies, building on specific areas described in their respective curricula. These plans include detailed curriculum implementation actions as well as resources to help schools.

Another approach used by countries is to take certain curricular development measures to help extend the existing curriculum. Examples that focus on the importance of the social and physical environment of students include Canada's Joint Consortium for School Health (JCSH).

Formal teacher education and training

Effective digital and hybrid education requires specialised knowledge and competences. TALIS 2018 results indicate that teachers felt less confident about supporting student learning through the use of digital technology than they did about other teaching tasks (OECD, 2019[14]). Even less is known about teachers' digital proficiency and teaching in other areas (digital risks, misinformation, digital assessments) and more modern technologies (data literacy and data inquiry skills to make efficient use of Teaching and Learning Analytics [TLA], intelligent learning systems and other artificial intelligence [AI] technologies) (Ulferts, 2021[38]; Minea-Pic, 2020[39]). In addition, investigations are needed into the knowledge and skills that help teachers successfully combine offline and online teaching and learning, thus creating holistic hybrid and blended learning experiences. In the future, the TALIS Teacher Knowledge Survey (TKS) assessment module implemented in TALIS 2024 may shed some light on teachers' technological knowledge, in particular their technological pedagogical knowledge.

What we do know is that teachers who were trained in the use of ICT are also more likely to let students use ICT for projects or classwork (OECD, 2019[14]) on average across OECD countries. However, only 56% of teachers reported learning about the use of ICT for teaching as part of initial teacher preparation and 60% as part of professional development activities. The majority of lower secondary teachers reported not feeling well-prepared in this area and their need for professional development was among the highest. Little is known about the quality and effectiveness of such training opportunities.

Technologies are constantly evolving, providing new educational opportunities through learning analytics as well as social robots and smart technologies powered by AI. Thus, systems should give teachers training opportunities to frequently update their technology-related knowledge and competences. For instance, to make efficient use of Teaching and Learning Analytics (TLA), teachers now need data literacy and data inquiry skills (Ulferts, 2021[38]).

Technology can boost professional learning and exchange among teachers and schools, and the world outside. Digitalisation allows more cost-effective and flexible learning opportunities. A broad range of digital platforms and open educational resources are now available to support teachers' work. Massive open online courses (MOOCs) offer new modes of delivering education. Online communities offer new possibilities to expand and activate teachers' professional networks and promote knowledge co-creation and sharing, as well as professional collaboration. Digital solutions make the pooling and sharing of knowledge about effective practices gained in research and in classrooms easier. This helps promote the use of research and data in schools, and provides researchers with information from the field. Digitalisation has also generated new approaches to certifying and recognising skills (e.g. open badges, micro-credentials).

During the COVID-19 pandemic, governments have relied on new training programmes, courses, and self-learning tools to help teachers adapt to the challenges of remote or hybrid teaching. These digital opportunities have also been harnessed for professional learning (OECD, 2021[41]). Many systems have implemented professional learning communities and networks to enhance teachers' skills and expertise. More focus should be placed on scaling up bottom-up and teacher-led networks that have emerged during the pandemic (Minea-Pic, 2020[39]).

Despite the many advantages that digitalisation offers for teachers' professional learning, new challenges have arisen: first of all, insights into and regulation of the content, quality and effectiveness of MOOCs and online platforms and resources are limited. More knowledge is needed about the principles that should guide the design of effective professional networks online (e.g. blended learning communities seem to work better than purely online ones) (Minea-Pic, 2020[39]). Furthermore, online information can be quite scattered through multiple sources. Teachers often need to spend many hours looking for what is needed on the Internet. A solution for the latter challenge would be to create a "networks of networks" that is able to pool multiple resources into one single web location. There is also the open question of how emerging forms of certification can be recognised as part of official teacher professional development schemes and whether they matter for career progression and compensation.

The 21st Century Children Policy Questionnaire looked into some of these issues. Overall, the majority of the responses to the 21st Century Children Policy Questionnaire concentrated on professional development programmes to address both technological issues in the classroom and the social and emotional development of students. Sometimes the support is embedded within the school through the creation of teams with specialised roles. Examples include the Digital Technologies in Focus, delivered by the Australian Curriculum, Assessment and Reporting Authority (ACARA), which provides support to 160 disadvantaged schools with ICT curriculum officers. In France, a recent national body of educational psychologists (PsyEN) has been mobilised to better attend to the range of cognitive and social needs of students by collaborating with teachers and families.

On-site initiatives such as these provide opportunities for teachers at the same school to engage in active learning and experimentation. This allows for collective participation and sharing reflections. In addition, carefully developed online learning resources can also offer dynamic and flexible opportunities for teacher professional development. In particular, when resources are sustained, intense and backed by a dedicated training programme over time, they are more likely to have a bigger impact on the professional development of teachers (Garet et al., 2001[42]).

Massive Open Online Courses also provide ongoing professional development in digital skills. An example is Webwise in Ireland, which helps integrate Internet safety into teaching and learning. Innovative approaches to online learning are included as well. In Portugal, blended learning training courses are being introduced to help psychologists develop the attitudes and skills to support teachers in adopting intervention strategies in the classroom to prevent and inhibit disruptive and bullying behaviours.

The Australian Government has developed two comprehensive portals, the Digital Technologies Hub and the Student Well-being Hub, to provide quality-assured learning resources and activities to support implementation of the Australian Curriculum. Both initiatives target students, parents and school leaders, provide activities and events, and host new content and resources as they are developed. The Student Well-being Hub also links to the Bullying. No Way! website, which provides helpful information and advice about bullying and promotes the National Day of Action against Bullying and Violence. It also provides a link to the Australian Student Well-being Framework, a foundational document to support school communities in building positive and inclusive learning environments. The Framework is based on evidence that demonstrates the strong association between safety, well-being and learning.

In addition to formal education for teachers, there are also a variety of initiatives that work with teachers and other actors (e.g. parents, mental health professionals, etc.). These are illustrated in Table 1.3.

Table 1.3 Training for teachers, parents and other actors

	Target group	Aims and methods
Ireland	Primary and post-primary teachers	Training in restorative practice, as an evidence-based approach to address bullying
Portugal	Psychologists in public schools	Develop attitudes and skills to support teachers in adopting strategies of intervention in the classroom to prevent and inhibit disruptive and bullying behaviours
		Develop attitudes and skills that will allow them to develop their relationship with early childhood education and care (ECEC) and first cycle teachers
Scotland (United Kingdom)	Teachers and educators	Training through Career-Long Professional Learning (CLPL) for working in partnership with families and to develop capacity and resilience skills for young people and all those who play a role in their lives to prevent and deal with bullying
Turkey	Parents	Address family and peer relationship issues and stress as well as issues related to anxiety over grade progression

Source: 21st Century Children Policy Questionnaire, see Burns, T. and F. Gottschalk (eds.) (2019), *Educating 21st Century Children: Emotional Well-being in the Digital Age*, Educational Research and Innovation, OECD Publishing, Paris, available at https://doi.org/10.1787/b7f33425-en (accessed on 1 April 2022).

Network approaches to teaching and learning

Networks play a key role in the development of coherent pedagogical approaches, support materials, professional sharing and learning, and leadership (Paniagua and Istance, 2018[30]). Networks can build upon whole school communities, but also on individuals from a diverse range of organisations, and extend their professional peer network beyond their own school. These peer networks can provide fresh eyes to reflect on the particular school culture and the way the community approaches their students' needs.

When providing examples of promising networks, some countries highlighted the important role of existing networks of schools to advance and improve teacher practices and professional learning. In the case of *Person@lize* in the Netherlands, four school boards and 18 schools from both primary and secondary education collaborate to learn from each other and inspire each other. The overall aim is to connect with individual learning needs and achieve better learning outcomes by focusing on personalised learning experiences.

Other networks and collaborations target specific practices, for example, using social and emotional skills and arts as a way to promote children and young people's well-being. The Student Success Network's (New York, United States) philosophy is that students need more than academic skills to realise their potential, and that social and emotional learning is essential to prepare them for success in life. Defining themselves as a movement, members of the network range from social entrepreneurial organisations, such as I-Mentor and Citizen Schools, to long-standing community-based organisations, such as the YMCA and Good Shepard Services. Organisations like Ramapo for Children serve students with special needs (Olson, 2018[43]). In order to build up the movement, they provide training sessions for creating workshops among their members and organise events. They have also developed an online platform to strengthen the sharing of resources and collaboration. Key partners at New York University's Research Alliance for New York City Schools help improve the quality of the data gathered and its use.

Partnerships with digital experts

Fostering digital skills and incorporating ICTs in the classroom involves more than simply trading textbooks for tablets. It raises the challenge of unprecedented investment in education technology and professional development so that teachers understand the use, content and pedagogical implications of technology. Further, it implies establishing stronger connections with the whole community for most of the opportunities and challenges that come with the use of technology both inside and outside the school. Therefore, comprehensive efforts to bring families and community organisations together are needed to ensure digital learning does not become another source of disadvantage (Hooft Graafland, 2018[44]).

Despite the growing emphasis on equipping teachers with digital competences, countries reported few partnerships with programmers and experts in cybersecurity. This is potentially due to a number of factors. Firstly, areas of programming/coding and cybersecurity are not among the key priorities of education policy makers despite the attention paid to protecting children from online risks. Furthermore, teachers are often expected to integrate digital skills into existing subjects. This would be a powerful way forward if teachers were proficient in these skills. This does not seems to be the case, however, as highlighted by the lack of access to teacher training in these subjects mentioned earlier.

Schools that are successful in using technology effectively establish strong partnerships with key stakeholders from universities, technology companies and other organisations. This is not always straightforward as it can involve actors with conflicting agendas, which can undermine healthy collaborations. The formation of partnerships with private sector companies (for example, cyber security experts or representatives of large platforms/service providers such as Google or Microsoft) can be particularly challenging, given the different agendas and expectations of the sectors. However, given the speed of technological change, a way for these actors to work together must be found. This is especially true given the decentralised nature of many education systems, which effectively locates the responsibility for protecting student data and ensuring the security of school and class technology infrastructure to schools.

A variety of examples of effective partnerships were provided in the Policy Questionnaire responses. For example, in New Brunswick and Nova Scotia (Canada), Brilliant Labs, a not-for-profit technology and experiential learning platform, collaborates with schools to implement Makerspaces. These labs build on the pedagogical approach of 'Maker Culture'. It encourages learners to use, explore and experiment with diverse materials and tools to build engines and complex tools. This creates an authentic learning experience that activates previous Science, Technology, Engineering, Art and Mathematics (STEAM) knowledge. Brilliant Lab's makerspaces are managed by their staff, who support the design of the space and professional development. Schools determine the equipment needed and accordingly leverage their traditional funding sources and practices. The success of this partnership is illustrated by how the maker movement is being implemented in hundreds of schools across Atlantic Canada. Their 'platform' nature encourages and prepares schools to deliver maker opportunities rather than just a one-off service (MakerMedia, 2019[45]).

Although more focused on providing infrastructure, the ambitious pilot initiative launched by the Greek Ministry of Education is similar in that it has implemented a network of 145 open technology laboratories across the country in partnership with Building Infrastructure and the National Bank's i-bank. The labs consist of a network of workstations with Raspberry Pi computers, robotics kits, 3D printers and scanners, interactive projectors, multifunction peripherals and various sensors. The aim is that the network will develop into a broader professional community of practice around the effective use of ICTs.

Other actions revolve around supporting partnerships for the professional development of teachers. In Ireland, the *Schools Excellence Fund – Digital* invites clusters of 4-6 schools to work together on innovative projects in teaching and learning using digital technologies. These clusters can receive up to EUR 30 000 to run a project over a three-year period. Examples include a cluster of six post-primary schools in Dublin, Cork and Westmeath, working together on a project that will use drones to record footage of the local areas to inform core elements of the Junior and Senior Cycle Geography curricula, while another cluster of Midlands post-primary schools are using industry-lead training in MoJo (mobile journalism) video content creation to enhance teaching, learning and digital literacy among educators and students in the cluster schools (DES, 2018).

SOME CONCLUSIONS

We need to include the voices of children

The conclusions of this chapter are drawn from *Educating 21st Century Children: Emotional Well-being in the Digital Age* (Burns and Gottschalk, 2019[29]) as well as *Education in the Digital Age: Healthy and Happy Children* (Burns and Gottschalk, 2020[45]). Children are active users of digital technologies, and one of their preferred activities is information seeking, whether for socialisation, searching for health information or schoolwork. In respecting student rights and agency, education supports the development of strong critical thinking and media literacy skills that empower children to be well-informed agents of change. We have seen the impact of organised youth activism in terms of the global climate change protests. Student voices focus attention on the positive opportunities digital technologies afford (rather than risks, which is common in the current adult-centred research and policy discourse). These are just some of the ways in which empowered children and youth contribute to shaping the world they will inherit.

Children and youth tend to be early adopters of new digital technologies and they are also the group most targeted by digital software developers and platforms. Although it is often assumed that children and youth do not understand or do not care about their digital privacy, recent research indicates that they have a fluid understanding of their privacy, valuing specific elements over others and choosing when and where to reveal data about themselves (Burns and Gottschalk, 2019[29]; Burns and Gottschalk, 2020[45]). They may also sometimes choose to prioritise popularity (measured by the number of likes or shares on certain apps, for example) over privacy. In general, children and youth are becoming more critical and shrewder about what they see in the digital environment. This does not mean that they do not need protection or help with cyber risks, especially the youngest children. But it does imply that the type of help needed could be adapted and targeted better, taking children's own agency into account. This also extends to the physical environment, where children are, for example, increasingly included in discussions of play space design and broader urban planning discussions, as well as the development of inclusive health and well-being education programmes.

We need to adequately support our teachers

Teachers are increasingly expected to help integrate students of different backgrounds; to be sensitive to cultural, linguistic and gender issues; to encourage tolerance and cohesion; to respond effectively to the needs of all students; and at the same time encourage them to be self-directed learners. Teachers are also expected to prepare students for the digital world and accompanying (and rapidly evolving) knowledge and skill sets. As highlighted by the COVID-19 pandemic, they are also increasingly expected to help develop healthy habits and monitor physical and emotional well-being. All of these tasks require specific knowledge, competencies and skills. As systems increasingly recognise the need to prepare teachers for this diverse set of roles, there must be greater effort to update and ensure the quality of initial teacher education and ongoing professional development. There is also a need to better connect the stages of teacher education, improve the alignment of the various stages, and ensure that high-quality and targeted support is available when most needed.

We need to build and reinforce partnerships with other sectors

Ensuring student well-being in a digital world means that schools are increasingly expected to work in partnership with other actors. These include parents and families, but also health professionals, psychologists and law enforcement. Increasingly, they also include digital experts, cyber security professionals and programmers (Burns and Gottschalk, 2019[29]; Burns and Gottschalk, 2020[45]). Developing and maintaining partnerships with such a diverse set of actors, some of whom (for example those from the private sector) have different aims and goals, is a complex challenge. Although, historically, public and private partnerships have been limited in many systems, the speed of change of digital technology makes it imperative to connect to the private sector where the majority of tech firms are concentrated.

This has a number of repercussions, including thinking through what this means for the protection of education as a public good and how to build capacity across the system from the central ministry to the classroom, to continuously learn and evolve digital competencies along with technological change. In addition, as much of the directly measured digital use data and content (i.e. from user behaviour) is owned by private companies such as social media platforms and other providers, there is also a need for agreement on sharing data and measurements for policy and research purposes, as well as regulated restrictions on collecting and using such data.

REFERENCES

Arnold, K. and M. Pistilli (2012), "Course signals at Purdue", *Proceedings of the 2nd International Conference on Learning Analytics and Knowledge,* https://doi.org/10.1145/2330601.2330666. [9]

Asbell-Clarke, J. et al. (2020), "The Importance of Teacher Bridging in Game-Based Learning Classrooms", in *Global Perspectives on Gameful and Playful Teaching and Learning, Advances in Educational Technologies and Instructional Design,* IGI Global, https://doi.org/10.4018/978-1-7998-2015-4.ch010. [10]

Baker, R. (2016), "Stupid Tutoring Systems, Intelligent Humans", *International Journal of Artificial Intelligence in Education,* Vol. 26/2, pp. 600-614, https://doi.org/10.1007/s40593-016-0105-0. [3]

Biesta, G. (2015), *Good Education in an Age of Measurement: Ethics, Politics, Democracy,* Routledge. [20]

Burns, T. and F. Gottschalk (eds.) (2020), *Education in the Digital Age: Healthy and Happy Children,* Educational Research and Innovation, OECD Publishing, Paris, https://dx.doi.org/10.1787/1209166a-en. [45]

Burns, T. and F. Gottschalk (eds.) (2019), *Educating 21st Century Children: Emotional Well-being in the Digital Age,* Educational Research and Innovation, OECD Publishing, Paris, https://dx.doi.org/10.1787/b7f33425-en. [29]

Byrne, J. et al. (2016), *Global Kids Online Research Synthesis, 2015-2016.* [15]

Council of Europe (2019), *Digital Citizenship Education Handbook,* Council of Europe Publishing, Strasbourg. [13]

DeFalco, J. et al. (2017), "Detecting and Addressing Frustration in a Serious Game for Military Training", *International Journal of Artificial Intelligence in Education,* Vol. 28/2, pp. 152-193, https://doi.org/10.1007/s40593-017-0152-1. [7]

Garet, M. et al. (2001), "What Makes Professional Development Effective? Results From a National Sample of Teachers", *American Educational Research Journal,* Vol. 38/4, pp. 915-945, https://doi.org/10.3102/00028312038004915. [41]

Good, J. (2021), *Serving students with special needs better: How digital technology can help,* OECD Publishing, Paris. [25]

Hargittai, E. (2002), "Second-level digital divide: Differences in people's online skills", *First Monday,* Vol. 7/4, https://doi.org/10.5210/fm.v7i4.942. [34]

Helsper, E., A. Van Deursen and R. Eynon (2015), *Tangible Outcomes of Internet Use: From Digital Skills to Tangible Outcomes project report,* http://www.oii.ox.ac.uk/research/projects/?id=112. [22]

Hooft Graafland, J. (2018), "New technologies and 21st century children: Recent trends and outcomes", *OECD Education Working Papers,* No. 179, OECD Publishing, Paris, https://dx.doi.org/10.1787/e071a505-en. [43]

Karumbaiah, S., J. Ocumpaugh and R. Baker (2019), *The Influence of School Demographics on the Relationship Between Students' Help-Seeking Behavior and Performance and Motivational Measures.* [27]

Kizilcec, R. et al. (2017), "Closing global achievement gaps in MOOCs", *Science,* Vol. 355/6322, pp. 251-252, https://doi.org/10.1126/science.aag2063. [8]

Law, N., A. Yuen and R. Fox (2011), *Educational Innovations Beyond Technology,* Springer US, Boston, MA, https://doi.org/10.1007/978-0-387-71148-5. [23]

Livingstone, S. et al. (2011), *EU Kids Online: Final Report 2011*, EU Kids Online, London, http://eprints.lse.ac.uk/id/eprint/45490. [18]

MakerMedia (2019), *Brilliant Labs: Building Creativity, Innovation and Entrepreneurship in Atlantic Canada,* http://newsletter.makermedia.com/dm?id=D3EDCF73556229037244AE6816EC8451&fbclid=IwAR24ecZUsFY3rODLE2teO7D8TQ-8aVWTdF1ajcLv5WRh0ayWThKiaSNvzds. [44]

Mascheroni, G. and K. Ólafsson (2016), "The mobile Internet: Access, use, opportunities and divides among European children", *New Media & Society,* Vol. 18/8, pp. 1657-1679, https://doi.org/10.1177/1461444814567986. [35]

Minea-Pic, A. (2020), "Innovating teachers' professional learning through digital technologies", *OECD Education Working Papers,* No. 237, OECD Publishing, Paris, https://dx.doi.org/10.1787/3329fae9-en. [39]

Molenaar, I. (2021), *Personalisation of learning: Towards hybrid human-AI learning technologies,* OECD Publishing, Paris. [6]

Ocumpaugh, J. et al. (2014), "Population validity for educational data mining models: A case study in affect detection", *British Journal of Educational Technology,* Vol. 45/3, pp. 487-501, https://doi.org/10.1111/bjet.12156. [26]

OECD (2021), *OECD Digital Education Outlook 2021: Pushing the Frontiers with Artificial Intelligence, Blockchain and Robots,* OECD Publishing, Paris, https://dx.doi.org/10.1787/589b283f-en. [1]

OECD (2021), *The State of School Education: One Year into the COVID Pandemic,* OECD Publishing, Paris, https://dx.doi.org/10.1787/201dde84-en. [40]

OECD (2019), *Going Digital: Shaping Policies, Improving Lives,* OECD Publishing, Paris, https://dx.doi.org/10.1787/9789264312012-en. [5]

OECD (2019), *TALIS 2018 Results (Volume I): Teachers and School Leaders as Lifelong Learners,* TALIS, OECD Publishing, Paris, https://dx.doi.org/10.1787/1d0bc92a-en. [14]

OECD (2018), "A brave new world: Technology and education", *Trends Shaping Education Spotlights*, No. 15, OECD Publishing, Paris, https://dx.doi.org/10.1787/9b181d3c-en. [19]

OECD (2017), *PISA 2015 Results (Volume III): Students' Well-Being,* PISA, OECD Publishing, Paris, https://dx.doi.org/10.1787/9789264273856-en. [16]

OECD (2014), *TALIS 2013 Results: An International Perspective on Teaching and Learning,* TALIS, OECD Publishing, Paris, https://dx.doi.org/10.1787/9789264196261-en. [31]

OECD (2010), *Educating Teachers for Diversity: Meeting the Challenge,* OECD Publishing, Paris, https://doi.org/10.1787/20769679. [37]

Olson, L. (2018), *School-community Partnerships: Joining Forces to Support the Learning and Development of All Students,* https://assets.aspeninstitute.org/content/uploads/2018/04/Community-School-Partnerships-Case-Study.pdf?_ga=2.161057341.1885640925.1554812794-1915899689.1554373626. [42]

P. Kampylis, N. (ed.) (2013), *Towards a policy framework for understanding and upscaling ICT-enabled learning innovations: Synthesis and Conclusions*, Publications Office of the European Union, Luxembourg. [24]

Pangrazio, L. (2014), "Reconceptualising critical digital literacy", *Discourse: Studies in the Cultural Politics of Education*, Vol. 37/2, pp. 163-174, https://doi.org/10.1080/01596306.2014.942836. [21]

Paniagua, A. and D. Istance (2018), *Teachers as Designers of Learning Environments: The Importance of Innovative Pedagogies*, Educational Research and Innovation, OECD Publishing, Paris, https://dx.doi.org/10.1787/9789264085374-en. [30]

Park, E. and M. Kwon (2018), "Health-related internet use by children and adolescents: Systematic review", *Journal of Medical Internet Research*, Vol. 20/4, p. e120, https://doi.org/10.2196/jmir.7731. [28]

Pedró, F. et al. (2019), "Artificial intelligence in education: Challenges and opportunities for sustainable development", UNESCO, Paris, https://unesdoc.unesco.org/ark:/48223/pf0000366994. [4]

Ribble, M., G. Bailey and T. Ross (2004), "Digital citizenship: Addressing appropriate technology behavior", *Learning & Leading with technology*, Vol. 32/1, p. 6, https://eric.ed.gov/?id=EJ695788. [11]

Rutter, M. (2007), "Resilience, competence, and coping", *Child Abuse & Neglect*, Vol. 31/3, pp. 205-209, https://doi.org/10.1016/J.CHIABU.2007.02.001. [17]

Ulferts, H. (ed.) (2021), *Teaching as a Knowledge Profession: Studying Pedagogical Knowledge across Education Systems*, Educational Research and Innovation, OECD Publishing, Paris, https://dx.doi.org/10.1787/e823ef6e-en. [38]

UNICEF (2017), *The State of the World's Children: Children in a Digital World*, http://www.soapbox.co.uk. [12]

Valtonen, T. et al. (2015), "Developing a TPACK measurement instrument for 21st century pre-service teachers", *Seminar.net International Journal of Media, Technology & Lifelong Learning*, Vol. 11/2, https://journals.hioa.no/index.php/seminar/article/view/2353. [32]

Van Deursen, A. and E. Helsper (2018), "Collateral benefits of Internet use: Explaining the diverse outcomes of engaging with the Internet", *New Media & Society*, Vol. 20/7, pp. 2333-2351, https://doi.org/10.1177/1461444817715282. [36]

Van Dijk, J. (2017), "Digital divide: Impact of access", in *The International Encyclopedia of Media Effects*, John Wiley & Sons, Inc., https://doi.org/10.1002/9781118783764.wbieme0043. [33]

Wenger, E. (1987), *Artificial intelligence and tutoring systems: computational and cognitive approaches to the communication of knowledge*, Morgan Kaufmann Publishers Inc. [2]

02
SCHOOL SYSTEMS AS DRIVERS OF MORE INCLUSIVE COMMUNITIES

Schoolchildren have generally been less vulnerable to coronavirus than other demographic groups, yet they have been hard hit by policy responses to contain this virus: in 2020, 1.5 billion students in 188 countries were locked out of their schools. Some were able to continue their schooling through alternative learning opportunities, well-supported by their parents and teachers. However, many – particularly those from the most marginalised groups – had their schooling cut short as they did not have access to digital learning resources or lacked the support or motivation to learn on their own. The learning losses following these school closures may cast a long shadow over the economic well-being of individuals and nations.

The pandemic has exposed many inadequacies and inequities in our school systems – from the broadband and computers needed for online education to the supportive environments needed to focus on learning. There have also been central government failures in jumpstarting local initiatives and aligning resources with needs. Still, the pandemic has shown how schools can innovate when they have to. Teachers, parents and students can work together on new forms of learning and ways to protect public health.

This chapter looks at the consequences of excluding vulnerable groups in education. Lower learning outcomes translate into lower labour market outcomes (income, participation, etc.) and well-being (from social outcomes to mental and physical health).

These issues often affect societal outcomes more broadly: lower productivity, GDP, and tax revenues for countries, and increased welfare and social spending (e.g. with social welfare contributions). In conclusion, removing the barriers to education that these students face can bring positive outcomes for them and for their countries too. Teachers have a key role in implementing inclusive practices.

INCLUSIVE EDUCATION

Inclusive education has become a key concept in education over the last few decades. It has been the subject of international debate since UNESCO's 1994 Salamanca Declaration. Inclusion is defined as a process that helps overcome barriers to the presence, participation and achievement of all learners, irrespective of their personal characteristics (UNESCO, 2009[1]). It is about changing the system to fit the student, not changing the student to fit the system (UNICEF, 2014[2]).

The **OECD Strength through Diversity Project** defines inclusive education as *"an on going process aimed at offering quality education for all while respecting diversity and the different needs and abilities, characteristics and learning expectations of the students and communities, eliminating all forms of discrimination"* (UNESCO, 2009[1]).

Inclusive education is a dynamic process that is constantly evolving according to the local culture and context. It seeks to enable communities, systems and structures to combat discrimination, celebrate diversity, promote participation and overcome barriers to learning and participation for all people. All personal differences (i.e. age, gender, ethnicity, Indigenous status, language, health status, etc.) are acknowledged and respected. Today, inclusive education is generally viewed as "a matter of adopting a socio-ecological approach regarding the interactions between students' capabilities and environmental demands, stressing that educational systems must adapt to and reach all students – and not vice versa" (Amor et al., 2018[3]).

THE BENEFITS OF INCLUSIVE EDUCATION

The rationale behind inclusive education is partly grounded in human rights. But inclusive education also has an economic rationale. Education is correlated to most of the key life outcomes of an individual: employment, earnings, poverty levels, physical and mental health, well-being, social mobility, criminality and more (OECD, 2012[4]; Hanushek and Woessmann, 2007[5]; Hanushek and Woessmann, 2020[6]).

At the aggregate level, the level and quality of education that individuals receive have an impact on society in terms of increased GDP[1] growth, reduced healthcare costs and social spending, and improved social cohesion (OECD, 2006[7]).

Inclusive education provides benefits for all students in improving the quality of education offered. It is more child-centred and focused on achieving good learning outcomes for all students, including those with a diverse range of abilities (UNESCO, 2009[1]). Inclusive education can also foster students' socio-emotional growth, self-esteem and peer acceptance while helping to fight stigma, stereotyping, discrimination and alienation in schools and societies more broadly (UNESCO, 2020[8]). Another common argument in favour of inclusive education is an economic one: poverty reduction through improved education of disadvantaged students (UNICEF, 2014[2]).

Nevertheless, research and estimates on the potential gains and costs of reforms of inclusive education are limited. As an alternative to cost-benefit analyses, certain proxies can capture the advantages and benefits of a shift to more inclusive education systems. For instance, they can consider the personal and societal losses incurred due to the poor outcomes of diverse students in non-inclusive systems. Indeed, diverse groups of students often face challenges in mainstream education systems that lower their achievement and hinder their potential, and frequently report lower levels of social and emotional well-being in relation to their school experience (Brussino, 2020[9]; Rutigliano, 2020[10]; Mezzanotte, 2020[11]). Such barriers can relate to gender, geographical location, socio-economic status, disability, ethnicity, language, migration, displacement, incarceration, sexual orientation, gender identity and expression, religion, and other beliefs and attitudes. However, there are also costs associated with reforms towards inclusive education in terms of personnel and resources. The efficiency of these investments is often under scrutiny due to the lack of evidence on the effectiveness of these interventions.

Some groups of students are particularly impacted by non-inclusive practices and can become further marginalised in education. Even if there is currently very limited causal evidence on the impact of inclusive settings on students and societies, it is possible to identify the limits encountered when teaching diverse students in mainstream educational settings. Furthermore, the literature shows that educational outcomes affect a variety of later-life outcomes, such as employment rates, income levels, health, trust in government and political participation; removing barriers that constrain diverse students' outcomes is key. This is, by definition, the scope of inclusive educational reform, which aims for all students to learn to the best of their capabilities and with the best possible support for their individual needs.

Different relevant outcomes have been grouped as shown in Figure 2.1: academic, economic, social and societal outcomes. **Academic outcomes** encompass students' grade point averages (GPAs), credits, secondary graduation rates, tertiary enrolment and graduation rates, but also levels of engagement, absenteeism and early dropout. **Social outcomes** include social inclusion, friendship development and sense of belonging, but also experience of harassment, feelings of unsafety, discrimination, threats and violence. **Economic outcomes** cover employment and unemployment rates, earnings and wages, dependency on social grants, mental and physical health. **Societal outcomes** encompass productivity losses, production rates, levels of income taxes and social security contributions, and public expenditure levels.

From a governmental perspective, concerns about the financial sustainability of the education system are of paramount importance. According to the European Agency for Special Needs and Inclusive Education (2018[12]), one of the main reasons for financing inclusive education is to prevent exclusionary strategies; such approaches may deny learners their right to quality education and consequently lead to increasing expenditure in education.

Estimating potential gains resulting from improved inclusion in education and within society presents several challenges, from estimation of current losses of student potential to the most affected categories of students, and the limited availability of relevant data. Basic estimates exist about the gains that OECD countries could obtain by improving the academic outcomes of their low-performing students. For instance, in 2010 the OECD estimated enormous economic gains in improving the cognitive skills of OECD populations (OECD, 2010[13]). The OECD reported that a modest goal of all OECD countries boosting their average PISA (Programme for International Student

Assessment) scores by 25 points over the next 20 years implied an aggregate gain of OECD GDP of USD 115 trillion (EUR 94.7 trillion) over the lifetime of the generation born in 2010. More ambitious goals, such as bringing all students to a minimal level of proficiency for the OECD (a PISA score of 400), would imply aggregate GDP increases of close to USD 200 trillion (EUR 164.78 trillion), according to historical growth relationships. Bringing all countries up to the OECD's best-performing education system in PISA in 2009 (Finland) would result in gains of around USD 260 trillion (EUR 214.21 trillion) (OECD, 2010[13]).

Figure 2.1 **Key life outcomes**

Source: Mezzanotte, C. (2022), "The social and economic rationale of inclusive education: An overview of the outcomes in education for diverse groups of students", *OECD Education Working Papers*, No. 263, OECD Publishing, Paris, https://dx.doi.org/10.1787/bff7a85d-en.

From a governmental perspective, concerns about the financial sustainability of the education system are of paramount importance. According to the European Agency for Special Needs and Inclusive Education (2018[12]), one of the main reasons for financing inclusive education is to prevent exclusionary strategies; such approaches may deny learners their right to quality education and consequently lead to increasing expenditure in education.

Estimating potential gains resulting from improved inclusion in education and within society presents several challenges, from estimation of current losses of student potential to the most affected categories of students, and the limited availability of relevant data. Basic estimates exist about the gains that OECD countries could obtain by improving the academic outcomes of their low-performing students. For instance, in 2010 the OECD estimated enormous economic gains in improving the cognitive skills of OECD populations, as outlined above (OECD, 2010[13]).

The costs of non-inclusive education

The following section shows that, on average, certain groups of students tend to be low performers or have lower academic outcomes. Supporting these groups specifically may help to increase the average outcomes of low performers, producing a gain for OECD countries. Additional studies exist on particular groups of students – explored more extensively in the following section – that identify more specifically the costs that societies incur by not supporting these populations. For instance, the lack of inclusion of individuals with attention-deficit hyperactivity disorder (ADHD) has an estimated cost of USD 67-116 billion (EUR 55.2-95.57 billion) annually in the United States, mainly due to the loss of workforce productivity (Biederman and Faraone, 2006[14]). Similarly, according to the World Bank, the fiscal benefits that would derive from including Roma individuals across Central and Eastern Europe and Balkans Countries amount annually to EUR 3.4-9.9 billion (World Bank Group, 2010[15]). Concerning gender gaps, Ferrant and Kolev (2016[16]) have estimated that the current level of discrimination is estimated to incur a loss of up to USD 12 trillion (EUR 9.89 trillion) or 16% of global income. For OECD countries especially, this loss was estimated at about USD 6 116 billion (EUR 5 038.93 billion) (ibid.).

It is also possible to capture the advantages and benefits of a shift to inclusive education for countries and societies in terms of personal and societal losses incurred due to the low outcomes of diverse students in non-inclusive systems. All groups of diverse students, and the intersections of these groups, have to face challenges in education that often lower their achievement and hinder their potential. Indeed, diverse groups of students, such as immigrant students (OECD, 2019[17]), ethnic minorities (Kao and Thompson, 2003[18]) or students with special education needs (SEN) (Brussino, 2020[9]), tend to achieve at lower levels compared to their more advantaged peers. In addition, they often report lower levels of social and emotional well-being in relation to their school experience.

Lack of inclusion can be based on gender, geographical location, socio-economic status, disability, ethnicity, language, migration, displacement, incarceration, sexual orientation, gender identity and expression, religion, and other beliefs and attitudes (UNESCO, 2020[8]). The lack of inclusion of these groups in education constitute a cost not only at the individual but also at the societal level. Inequities can hamper the educational achievement of specific population groups, which, as mentioned earlier, can determine their employment, health and life-long outcomes.

For instance, geographical segregation has a strong impact on students' outcomes: research has documented the connections between neighbourhood socio-economic status and child and adolescent outcomes, including links to behavioural problems, juvenile delinquency, academic achievement and health issues (McArdle and Acevedo-Garcia, 2017[19]). This is often the case of students from ethnic minorities, such as Black and Hispanic students in the United States or Roma students in Europe, who are often segregated into both racially isolated and high-poverty schools

(OECD, 2019[20]). The same discourse can apply to Indigenous students, such as Aboriginal Australians (Dean, 2018[21]). The range of economic and social effects that inclusive education can procure is wide and applies to very diverse groups of learners. Social inclusion is believed to be one of the positive outcomes of inclusive education both during children's school years and when they begin their adult lives. In the first instance, it is identified as short-term social inclusion through participation in school and out-of-school activities and in the second instance, it indicates the long-term forms of social inclusion, such as being employed and leading a social life. Moreover, from a review by Ruijs and Peetsma (2009[22]), it appears that students with special educational needs perform better academically in inclusive settings than in non-inclusive settings.

Research also shows that attending and receiving support within inclusive education settings can increase the likelihood of enrolling in higher education for students with SEN. These settings are also beneficial for students that have no disability or impairment since attending class alongside a student with SEN can yield positive outcomes for their social attitudes and beliefs (Abt Associates, 2016[23]). Similarly, with the inclusion in education of students from diverse ethnic groups and national minorities, young people have the opportunity, through repeated exposure and practice, to engage with others who differ from them. This interaction can relate to feelings of satisfaction and social efficacy within the current school setting and inform future social interactions and social adaptability in college, communities, and the workplace (Nishina et al., 2019[24]). As predicted by Contact Hypothesis (Allport, 1954[25]), increased inter-group contact could lead to a reduction of hostility, prejudice and discrimination between groups, which can refer to all types of diversity. Instead, a context that allows contact between diverse peers can build strong social skills, an important asset in today's diverse and international places of work. An instance where this cannot occur is the case of same-sex or single-sex schools. Such schools appear to increase the gender salience of students (i.e. the awareness of gender categorisation) and levels of anxiety on mixed-gender interactions, which can worsen the students' socio-psychological well-being. Moreover, these settings can increase gender stereotyping and legitimise institutionalised sexism (Halpern et al., 2011[26]).

Countries that have higher levels of gender equality in their societies, which also impact education systems, generally have smaller or no gender gaps in subjects in which boys traditionally outperform girls. From Guido and colleagues' analysis (2008[27]) and subsequent studies (Fryer and Levitt, 2010[28]), there appears to be a positive correlation between gender equality and gender gap in mathematics: cultures that are more gender-equal are associated with a reduction in the negative gap in mathematics.

A further dimension of inclusion in school is student well-being and mental health. In New Brunswick (Canada), children and youth take part every three years in a wellness survey, which examines student perceptions, attitudes, and behaviours in areas related to personal well-being. This survey consistently yields positive results (New Brunswick Health Council, 2019[29]). In 2019 specifically, 92% of students reported a high level of connectedness, 85% of students a high level of pro-social behaviour, including 81% of youth with special education needs reporting the same. In examining healthy and inclusive schools in New Brunswick, it appears that a sense of connectedness was foundational in schools that successfully implemented inclusive education (AuCoin, Porter and Baker-Korotkov, 2020[30]). Moreover, the system in New Brunswick appears to be highly successful in keeping students engaged, with a reported dropout rate of only 1.1% (New Brunswick Department of Education and Early Childhood Development, 2019[31]).

EFFECTS OF INCLUSION IN EDUCATION FOR DIFFERENT STUDENT GROUPS

Some groups of students are particularly impacted by non-inclusive practices and can become further marginalised in education. These groups are various and often intersect among each other, which results in even more complex needs and sources of discrimination.

This section analyses the barriers and challenges that diverse groups face in education systems in more detail, and the potential gains that they could obtain in inclusive education systems.

Students with special education needs (SEN)

Despite progress in most OECD countries over the last few decades, students with SEN still experience significant disparities in terms of enrolment, graduation and employment outcomes. Moreover, students with SEN tend to suffer from a lack of social inclusion and experience worse social and emotional outcomes compared to their peers.

Evidence from the Washington Group on Disability Statistics (WG) (Figure 2.2) shows that in OECD countries with reported data on university completion rates disaggregated by disability status, both male and female individuals with a disability have lower completion rates than their peers. In Canada, for instance, an average of 53% of males with disabilities complete university, against around 70% of males without disabilities (Washington Group on Disability Statistics, 2018[32]).

The literature has also shed light on the link between inclusive education and social inclusion, mediated by friendships and peer relationships developed in school (European Agency for Special Needs and Inclusive Education, 2018[33]). Regarding friendships and peer interactions in compulsory education, evidence shows that social interactions in inclusive settings are a prerequisite for the development of friendships and other social skills and behaviours (ibid.). Some studies show that inclusive education can provide the space for social interactions to take place, leading to the development of friendships, social and communication skills, support networks, a sense of belonging, and positive behavioural outcomes. Also, as education can provide individuals with the skills, experience and empowerment to vocalise their opinions, inclusion in education can be a first step towards increasing political participation and social justice for people with disabilities (Morgon Banks and Polack, 2015[34]). Therefore, inclusive education can improve individual and family well-being while encouraging greater acceptance of diversity and the development of more tolerant, equitable and cohesive societies (ibid.).

A possible pathway by which inclusion generates economic advantages for individuals, families and governments is presented in figure 2.3. The figure suggests that inclusion through various forms of personal improvement fosters greater participation in employment and other paid activities. This represents gains for individuals with SEN, their families and societies as a whole.

Figure 2.2 University completion rates disaggregated by disability status and gender

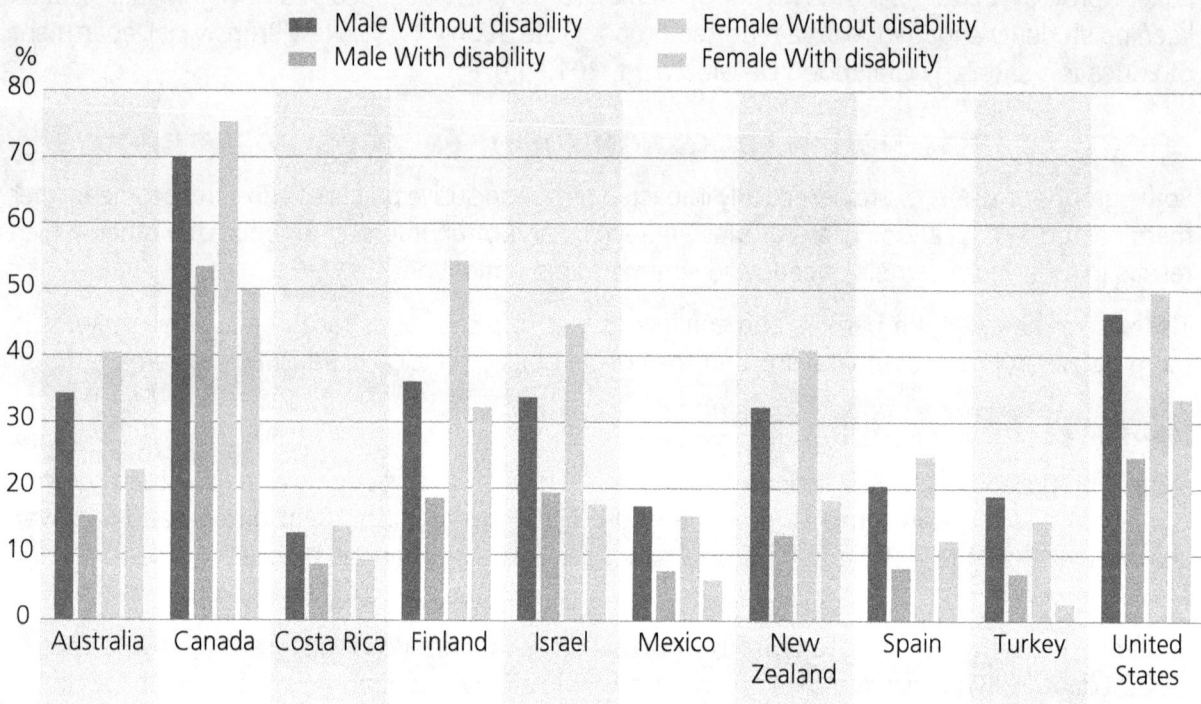

Note: University completion: percentage of a cohort of individuals who have completed an undergraduate university degree. All countries reported data for individuals aged 25-54 except Finland, which reported the data for people aged 29-64 years. The countries have been selected based on their status as Members of the OECD, from the countries reported by the Washington Group.
Source: Washington Group on Disability Statistics (2018[32]), *Selected SDG Indicators Disaggregated by Disability Status*, https://www.washingtongroup-disability.com/fileadmin/uploads/wg/Documents/Disagregation-Data-Report_.pdf (accessed 15 February 2020).

Gifted students

Data on gifted students is limited across OECD countries due to large variations in definitions, identification strategies and programmes to serve this population. Indeed, although giftedness is a term commonly used in research, there is no widely accepted definition, and assumptions about, and criteria for, giftedness differ between theoretical models. Despite these differences, a common feature is generally the recognition that there are multiple domains of giftedness: not only cognitive, but also artistic, athletic, etc. Moreover, access to gifted programming therefore varies by ethnicity, socio-economic level, locale and region. Studies have shown that gifted students can be significantly marginalised because, when they are not always high achievers, certain idiosyncrasies, such as unpredictable behaviour, are difficult to measure, and traditional and extrinsic motivators do not always work for them (Yarrison, 2018[35]). A common issue when discussing "intellectually gifted students" specifically is that of academic underachievement, although the literature disagrees on the concept of "underperforming gifted individuals" (Dowdall and Colangelo, 1982[36]).

Figure 2.3 Inclusive education pathways to economic gains

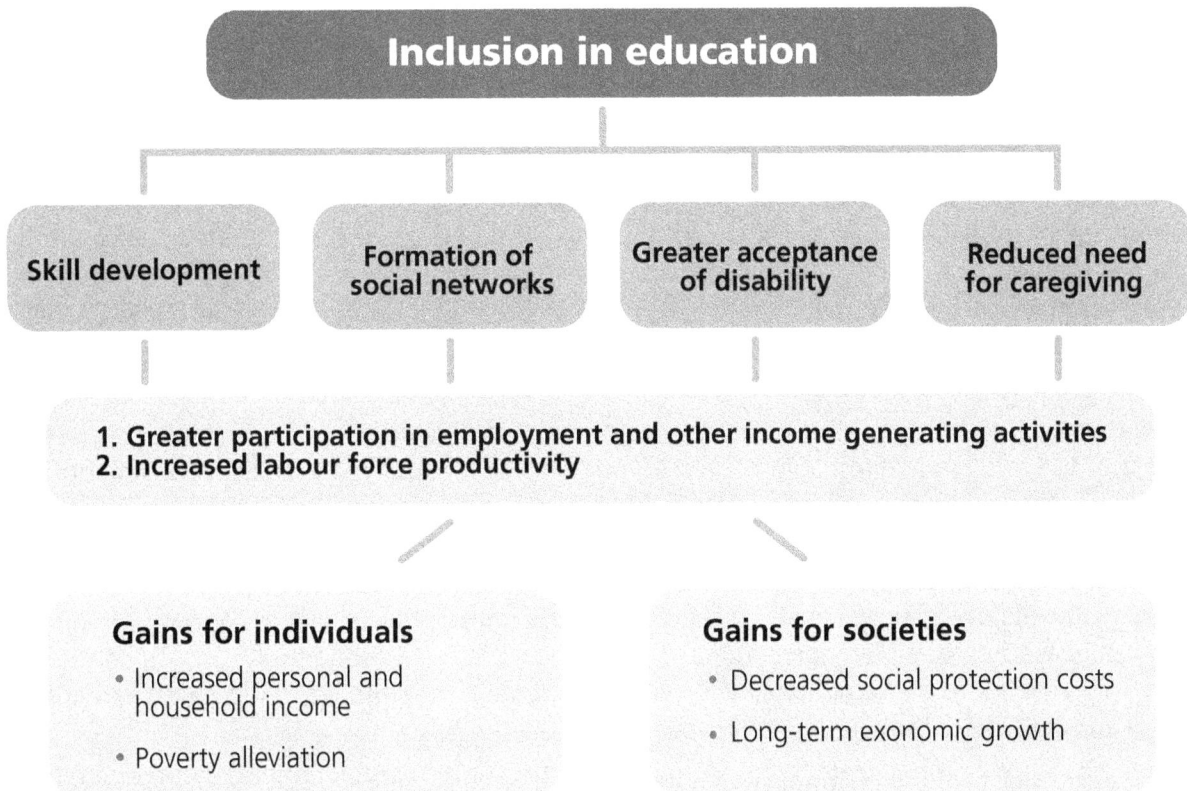

Source: Adapted in Mezzanotte (2022[75]) from Morgon, Banks and Polack (2015[34]), *The Economic Costs of Exclusion and Gains of Inclusion of People with Disabilities: Evidence from Low and Middle-Income Countries, International Centre for Evidence in Disability,* London School of Hygiene & Tropical Medicine, https://www.iapb.org/wp-content/uploads/CBM_Costs-of-Exclusion-and-Gains-of-Inclusion-Report_2015.pdf (accessed on 12 February 2021).

Moreover, access to gifted programming varies not only by country, but also by personal characteristics. For instance, ethnicity, socio economic level, locale and region appear to influence participation in gifted programmes within schools for different groups of students. Indeed, data from the United States show great variations in the percentage of students in public schools enrolled in gifted and talented programmes. Asian students between 2013 and 2014 were enrolled at significantly greater percentages (13.3%) into such programmes, compared to groups, such as Black (4.3%), Hispanic (4.9%) or Pacific Islander (4.4%). Moreover, differences also depend on the individual States, as in 2013-14 Kentucky and Maryland (15.8% and 16%) reported percentages of students enrolled in gifted programmes that were ten times those of Vermont or Massachusetts (0.3% and 0.7%).

Gifted underachievement is sometimes defined in literature as a frustrating loss of potential for society (Ritchotte, Matthews and Flowers, 2014[37]). Thus, there exists a societal reward for including these students in education and breaking down barriers for their achievement. Moreover, a more inclusive gifted education could "offer the possibility of cultivating a society's most promising talents into a source of exceptional human capital and creative capacity" (Heuser, Wang and Shahid, 2017[38]).

A report from the Employment, Workplace Relations, Small Business and Education References Committee of Australia from 2001 claims that support for gifted children in education contains a component of social equality (Senate Employment Workplace Relations, Small Business and Education References Committee, 2001[39]). Although gifted children are found in all socio-economic and ethnic groups, children from wealthier families benefit from more out-of-school support, while children from poorer families depend more on the school's provision. Untrained teachers are more likely to identify children of the dominant culture as gifted and well-behaved and less likely to notice giftedness among underachievers or minority groups. This suggests that more school support for the education of gifted students could contribute to balancing social inequity. For instance, in the State of Illinois (United States), the U-46 programme screens all students in third grade for the gifted classes of grades 4-6 to ensure that all students are considered for such programmes (U46, 2020[40]).

Immigrants and refugees

Educational opportunity is a major driving factor for many children and families who choose to migrate, but refugee and immigrant children frequently face multiple barriers to beginning and continuing their education, often due to restrictive migration policies (UNICEF, 2016[41]). The lack of specific skills, language and knowledge of the host country frequently hampers their integration and personal well-being (OECD, 2018[42]). Society's ability to maintain social cohesion in the presence of large migration flows depends on its capacity to integrate immigrants. Education can help immigrants and refugees to acquire skills and contribute to the host country's economy. It can also contribute to immigrants' social and emotional well-being, and sustain their motivation to participate in the social and civic life of their new communities (OECD, 2018[42]).

A further risk factor for immigrant students is segregation or isolation in specific schools. Isolation means that students with an immigrant background tend to be concentrated in schools where there is a higher-than-average share of immigrant students. PISA estimates an isolation index that illustrates the extent to which a student with an immigrant background is likely to be surrounded by immigrant students. The isolation index has a value close to 1 when immigrant students are concentrated in schools that non-immigrant students are unlikely to attend. Figure 2.4 shows that the isolation index of immigrant students is at 0.45 on average in OECD countries.

Further challenges to the inclusion of immigrant and refugee students depend on the school environment and the impact that it can have on their well-being and safety. Research indicates that these children are most likely to directly encounter discrimination in school settings, often in the form of insults, unfair treatment, exclusion and threats (UNICEF, 2016[41]). Children that suffer from these forms of social exclusion experience a range of repercussions such as distrust, hopelessness and problematic behaviour, as well as negative long-term attitudes about schooling and their own potential (Brown, 2015[44]). The social exclusion of these students can influence their academic outcomes, so that they perform worse academically, are at greater risk of dropping out and believe that doing well in school is neither important nor useful (ibid.). However, there exists evidence that suggests that interethnic contact is positively related to attitudes towards those from diverse backgrounds (Pettigrew and Tropp, 2006[45]). PISA 2018 also analyses the association between the proportion of immigrant students in school and students' attitudes towards immigrants. PISA finds positive and negative associations in different countries, which, according to the report, could indicate that a positive association between attitudes towards immigrants and the proportion of immigrant students in school is conditional on successful integration policies and the availability of resources to fund quality education for all (OECD, 2020[46]).

Figure 2.4 **Segregation of immigrant students across countries**

Index of isolation of immigrant students in school

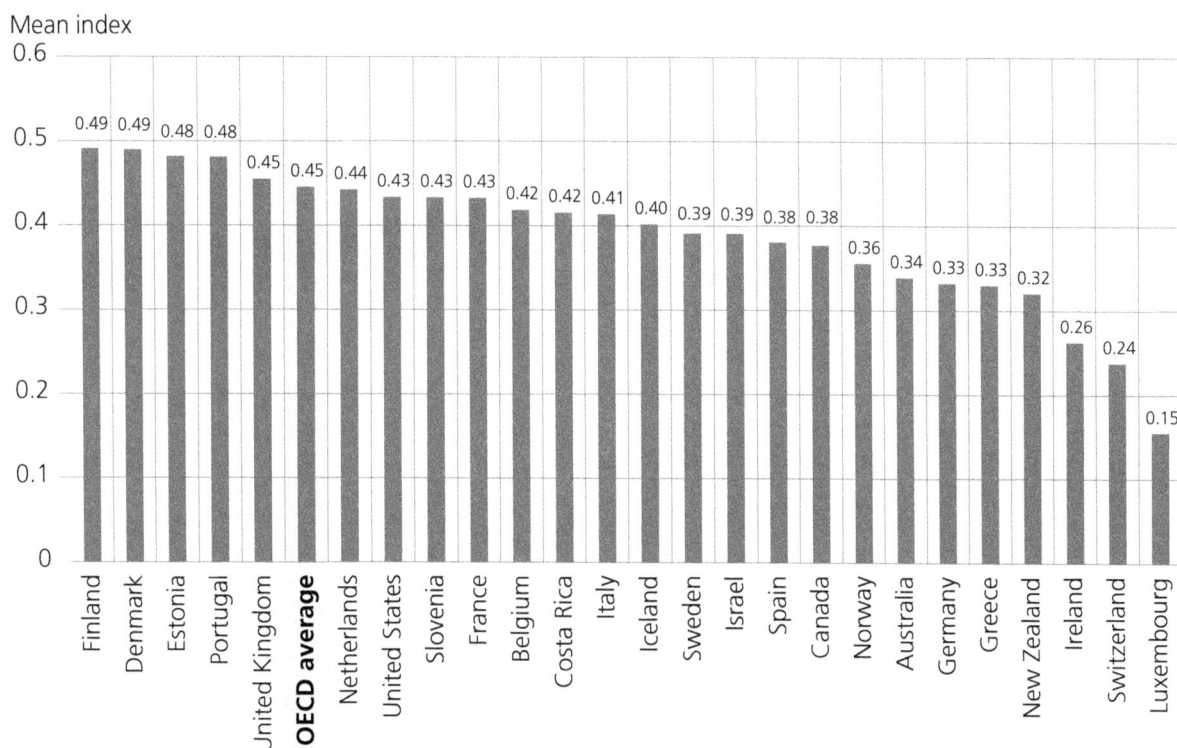

Mean index

0.6

0.5 0.49 0.49 0.48 0.48

0.45 0.45 0.44 0.43 0.43 0.43

0.42 0.42 0.41 0.40 0.39 0.39 0.38 0.38

0.36 0.34 0.33 0.33 0.32

0.26 0.24

0.15

Finland, Denmark, Estonia, Portugal, United Kingdom, **OECD average**, Netherlands, United States, Slovenia, France, Belgium, Costa Rica, Italy, Iceland, Sweden, Israel, Spain, Canada, Norway, Australia, Germany, Greece, New Zealand, Ireland, Switzerland, Luxembourg

Note: Countries where less than 5% of students had an immigrant background are not represented in the figure. The isolation index measures whether immigrant students are concentrated in some schools. The index is related to the likelihood of a representative immigrant student being enrolled in schools that enrol non-immigrant students. It ranges from 0 to 1, with 0 corresponding to no segregation and 1 to full.

Source: OECD (2018[43]), *PISA 2018 Database,* Table II.B1.9.11, http://www.oecd.org/pisa/data/2018database/ (accessed on 13 February 2020).

For refugee children specifically, challenges frequently include negative stereotypes and discrimination. Refugees are often subject to negative attitudes of the host population towards refugees.

Data on refugee students remains limited, but the United Nations estimates that worldwide only around half of child refugees are enrolled in primary school and less than a quarter of adolescents are enrolled in secondary school. Overall, a refugee child is five times more like to be excluded from school than a non-refugee. Globally, 91% of children attend primary school, whereas only 61% of refugee children do so. As refugee children become older, the challenges increase: only 23% of refugee adolescents are enrolled in secondary school, compared to 84% globally (UNHRC, 2017[47]).

Figure 2.5 Rates of schooling for refugee children and adolescents, globally

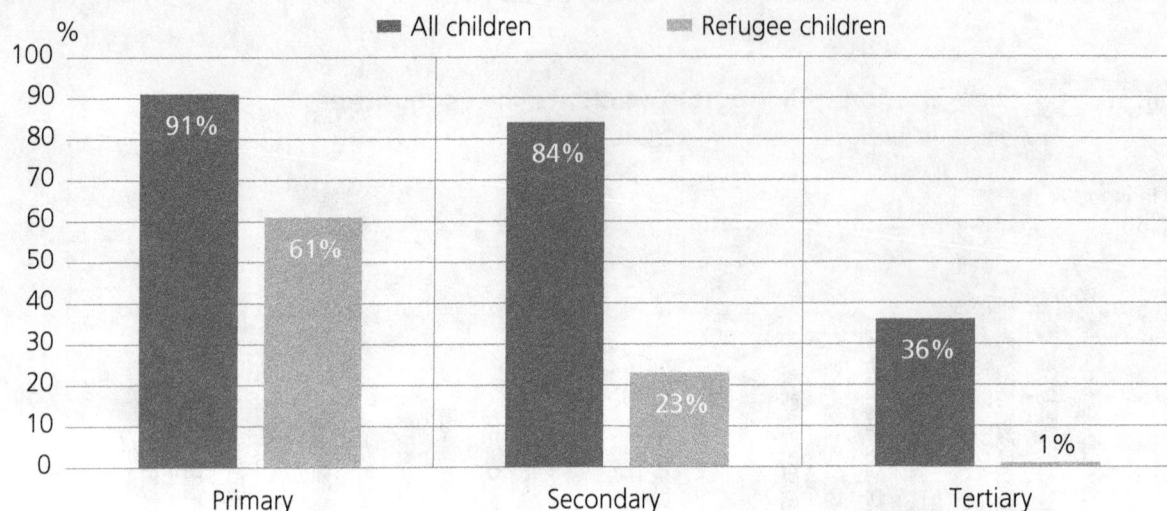

Note: The out-of-school rate for all adolescents refers to those of lower secondary school age (approximately 12-14 years), while the out-of-school rate for refugee adolescents refers to all those aged 12-17 years.
Source: UNHCR (2017[47]) *Left Behind: Refugee Education in Crisis,* https://www.unhcr.org/59b696f44.pdf (accessed on 10 June 2021).

While many OECD countries are making efforts to enrol newly arrived children in education, challenges still persist, especially for children from pre-primary and upper secondary ages who often fall out of national compulsory education systems (UNICEF, 2018[48]; Cerna, 2019[49]). In low-income countries, fewer than half of refugee children access primary education, and only 9% of refugee adolescents access secondary education in these countries (2017[47]).

Refugee girls, in particular, remain particularly disadvantaged: in primary school, for every ten refugee boys there are fewer than eight refugee girls. At secondary school the ratio is worse, with fewer than seven refugee girls for every ten refugee boys (2017[47]).

Although data on refugee children is limited, what is available reveals that refugee children face more obstacles than other children with an immigrant background (Cerna, 2019[49]). A variety of factors influence children's and their families' abilities to access education throughout the process of migration and displacement. For instance, as children move between regions or states, they may not have the legal right to attend school, especially if they have an irregular status. Moreover, they could face barriers due to a lack of language or social skills necessary for their inclusion in the host education system. When they settle in new locations, legal and language barriers, fear of immigration enforcement, inability to transfer their previous schoolwork and xenophobia are all common factors that keep children out of classrooms.

Ethnic groups, national minorities and Indigenous peoples

Given data collection and categorisation issues, it is challenging to make general and universal statements on the situation of individuals belonging to ethnic groups, national minorities and

Indigenous peoples in and beyond education. However, evidence exists from different countries on the conditions of students from specific ethnic groups or with an Indigenous background in education. For instance, Roma individuals represent the largest ethnic minority group in Europe and there are estimates regarding their situation, although the data collection entails several challenges. An OECD report on the Slovak Republic showed that Roma individuals tend to have lower educational attainment and higher dropout rates (OECD, 2019[20]). The reasons for this phenomenon are complex and context-specific, but usually include issues such as historically rooted discrimination, bullying, language barriers and misunderstood cultural variations within traditional education systems.

Data shows a pattern of continuous underachievement for certain ethnic groups. This trend starts with lower participation in early education, continues through further and higher education, and persists in the labour market. In the United States, where ethnicity data is reported more systematically than in most other OECD countries, it appears that achievement in education differs significantly between ethnic[2] groups. In European countries, too, there is data available on the gaps that students belonging to diverse ethnic groups and national minorities suffer. The group experiencing one of the largest academic gaps is Roma students (Rutigliano, 2020[10]). The percentage of Roma aged 16 to 64 who have completed upper secondary education remains below 15% across EU countries. The proportion is higher only in the Czech Republic (34%) and Slovakia (32%), but still far from the EU average of non-Roma individuals (European Union Agency for Fundamental Rights, 2017[50]).

The lack of inclusion in education affects the social inclusion that these groups experience later in life and the overall societal outcomes that are achieved. Roma populations are a striking case in point. Roma students' participation rates in early childhood education across Europe remain far below those of the population average while their dropout rates remain high (European Union Agency for Fundamental Rights, 2016, p. 27[51]).

Indigenous students suffer from similar challenges and limitations as ethnic and national minorities. In various OECD countries, Indigenous children generally have not had access to the same quality of education as other children in their country enjoy (OECD, 2017[52]). Indigenous children tend to have lower attendance rates, lower academic and socio-emotional outcomes, and higher dropout rates (Wannell and Currie, 2016[53]; Commonwealth of Australia, 2018[54]). Even in countries where the Indigenous population, such as the Māori and Pasifika in New Zealand, have steadily improved over the last decade, gaps remain with their non-Indigenous peers (Stats New Zealand, 2020[55]).

In Australia, poor educational outcomes are encountered at all levels of education for Indigenous students, from early childhood through to tertiary education. However, there have been improvements in educational participation and achievement in recent years; for example, Year 12's apparent retention rate increased from 38.0% in 2002 to 51.1% in 2012 for Indigenous students. There also appear to be substantial differences between the PISA scores of non-Indigenous students and Indigenous students, which can partially be explained by differences in background characteristics (such as socio-economic status) and schools attended. Yet data demonstrate the difficulty of reducing the gap in educational outcomes. While there have been absolute improvements in the educational performance of Indigenous students, general levels of education have also been increasing in non-Indigenous populations. Moreover, Indigenous people generally have lower rates of participation in the labour market, higher unemployment rates, higher poverty rates, limited access to housing, food insecurity and poor health levels compared to their non-Indigenous peers (Toulouse, 2016[56]; OECD, 2018[57]).

The inclusion of minority groups in education has an impact on other groups' development. As children go through their early life experiences, they form their attitudes and beliefs about other groups, which may be harder to change as they grow older. Young people must have opportunities to interact with members of other ethnic groups for meaningful cross-group bonds to develop. Diverse schools must offer more of these opportunities. Indeed, inclusive school environments are characterised by positive social experiences for all students, such as decreased bullying, reduced loneliness and greater numbers of cross-group friendships. A number of studies point to greater diversity predicting inclusivity in school, as measured by positive social experiences. More ethnically diverse schools (defined as schools that have many ethnic groups each with relatively even representation in the school) have students that feel safer, less bullied, less lonely and with less social anxiety compared with their same-ethnic counterparts in less diverse schools (Juvonen, Nishina and Graham, 2006[58]; Juvonen, Kogachi and Graham, 2017[59]). Moreover, studies on students in inclusive environments show that those who learn in such schools report greater interest in living and working in ethnically diverse environments when they become adults and are more likely to do so. In contrast, ethnically isolated schools may limit opportunities for young people to challenge skewed perceptions and assumptions about people from other racial groups (Tropp and Saxena, 2018[60]). Furthermore, there is mounting evidence that social interactions between groups has a positive impact on social cohesion, and particularly, trust. Research in the United States and Canada show that white people living in diverse neighbourhoods are more trusting when they regularly talk to their neighbours (Stolle, Soroka and Johnston, 2008[61]). This highlights not only the role stereotypes play in eroding social cohesion, but also the importance of social interactions to overcome them (OECD, 2020[62])

Gender

Gender is a well-documented factor of marginalisation in education. While 132 million girls are out of school globally (UNICEF, 2020[63]), OECD countries have made significant progress in narrowing or closing long-standing discrepancies in educational and job opportunities available to men and women. Yet gender differences remain in a number of areas throughout life: boys still tend to outperform girls in mathematics while girls outperform boys in reading. Furthermore, although more women than men now have a tertiary degree, women are still under-represented in better-paid fields, such as science and engineering. Women also face lower employment rates and tend to be paid less than similarly educated men (OECD, 2020[64]). However, the gradual closing of long-standing gaps in academic outcomes and beyond over the last few decades suggests that, if offered equal opportunities, boys and girls, men and women have equal chances of fulfilling their potential (OECD, 2015[65]).

Gender-based discrimination in education matters for economic growth. Previous empirical studies demonstrate that gender inequality in outcomes has a negative impact on growth, especially when it relates to gender disparities in education and labour (OECD, 2012[66]). The link between gender-responsive and inclusive education and improved learning outcomes, economic gains and country development, is indivisible (Diamond and Winfield, 2018[67]).

LGBTQI+ students

Students from the Lesbian, Gay, Bisexual, Transgender, Queer and Intersex (LGBTQI+) community suffer from a lack of inclusion in schools worldwide. LGBTQI+ students often deal with harassment, threats and violence directed at them daily (Human Rights Campaign, 2013[68]). Across the EU, nearly 60%

of LGBTQI+ respondents declared in 2019 that they have hidden their LGBTQI+ identity at school, and four in ten report having always or often experienced negative comments or conduct in the school setting because of their sexual orientation or identity (European Union Agency for Fundamental Rights, 2020[69]). Non-inclusive or hostile school settings are detrimental to the mental and physical health of LGBTQI+ youth and negatively affect educational attainment through lower participation in class or school activities, poorer academic performance and lower rates of attendance, or dropping out of school altogether (OECD, 2020[70]). This leads to lower learning outcomes and higher dropout or expulsion rates (Koehler et al., 2017[71]). Poor performance in school reduces opportunities for higher education and access to quality employment (ibid.).

Experiences of victimisation, such as bullying, can negatively affect LGBTQI+ youths' access to education as they are linked to increased absenteeism due to feeling uncomfortable or unsafe in school; increased discipline problems; and lower levels of school engagement and academic achievement (Kosciw et al., 2012[72]; Kosciw et al., 2010[73]).

Figure 2.6   **Perceived lack of safety at school by gender identity and sexual orientation**

Percentage of LGBTQI+ students who reported feeling unsafe based on sexual orientation, gender expression and gender (United States)

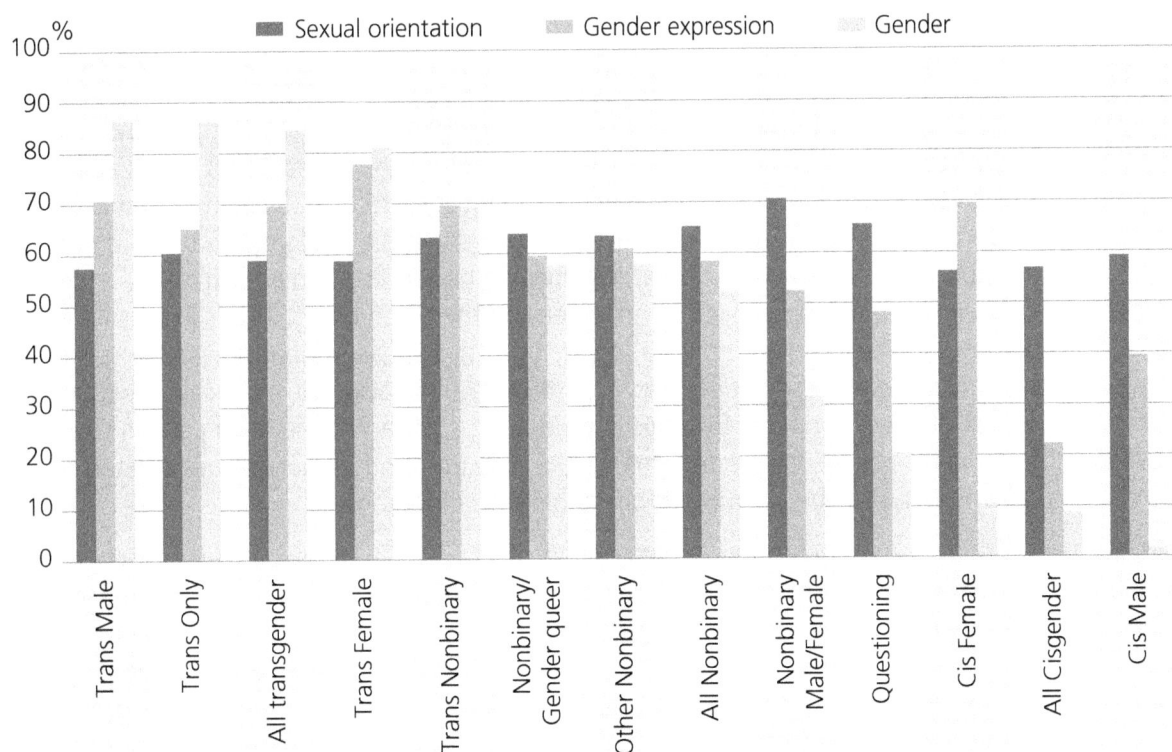

Source: Kosciw, J. G. et al. (2020[74]), *The 2019 National School Climate Survey: The experiences of lesbian, gay, bisexual, transgender, and queer youth in our nation's schools,* https://www.glsen.org/sites/default/files/2020-11/NSCS19-111820.pdf, (accessed 22 February 2021).

SOME CONCLUSIONS

The conclusions of this chapter are drawn from *The social and economic rationale of inclusive education* (Mezzanotte, 2022[75]), as well as *Building capacity for inclusive teaching* (Brussino, 2021[76]). Inclusion in education is a key condition for the achievement of sustainable, equitable and inclusive societies. It is an expression of societal justice, whatever the diversity of the people and children involved. Inclusion also has an economic rationale. Education is correlated to most of the key life outcomes of an individual: employment, earnings, poverty levels, physical and mental health, well-being, social mobility, criminality and more (OECD, 2012[4]; Hanushek and Woessmann, 2007[5]; Hanushek and Woessmann, 2020[6]). At the aggregate level, the level and quality of education that individuals receive have an impact on society in terms of increased GDP growth, reduced healthcare costs and social spending, and improved social cohesion (OECD, 2006[7]).

While inclusion in education started as a discourse on educating students with special education needs and catering to their needs so that they could achieve their potential in education and beyond, the quest for inclusive education continues much farther. All students require teaching methods and support mechanisms to help them to succeed and feel a sense of belonging at school and in society.

Inclusive education provides benefits for all students in improving the quality of education offered. It becomes more child-centred and focused on achieving good learning outcomes for all students, including those with a diverse range of abilities (UNESCO, 2009[1]). Inclusive education can also foster students' socio-emotional growth, self-esteem and peer acceptance, while helping to fight stigma, stereotyping, discrimination and alienation in schools and societies more broadly (UNESCO, 2020[8]).

Inclusive education is also an opportunity for improving students' quality of life, their future socio-economic outcomes and societal outcomes more broadly. Although research in this field is still limited, existing studies suggest that inclusion can bring positive outcomes. By compensating for the limitations of educational settings that nowadays impede vulnerable students' chances of success, countries can support their diverse populations in achieving better results in education, developing a higher sense of belonging to their societies and increasing their well-being. This is likely to improve societal outcomes and reduce governmental costs, due to decreased need for social spending. However, policy makers face specific challenges to further develop inclusion in education within their countries. The lack of relevant data, difficulties in estimating costs and benefits of potential reforms towards more inclusive education systems, intersectional issues, and the challenges created by the COVID-19 pandemic must all be accounted for in policy development.

Although educational inequalities often worsen during crises, COVID-19 has created new challenges as countries faced the dilemma of how to replace an education system built around physical schools. School closures have had a real impact on all students, but particularly so on the most vulnerable ones (OECD, 2020[77]). Diverse students have been particularly deprived of physical learning opportunities, social and emotional support available in schools and extra services. Learning losses experienced by students during the pandemic will subsequently reduce their earned income, recently estimated at 3%, while also implying lower rates of national economic growth (Hanushek and Woessmann, 2020[6]). According to Hanushek and Woessmann (ibid.), on the basis of historical data, a closure for one-third of a year could lower a country's GDP by an average of 1.5% over the remainder of the century.

Hanushek and Woessmann (Hanushek and Woessmann, 2020[6]) also note that, as vulnerable children have a harder time taking full advantage of remote learning, they could be more affected by the crisis than their peers. The crisis could therefore become an even larger burden in terms of equity of educational opportunities and outcomes and lead to further societal inequalities.

A further concern is the risk that education spending may decline in the coming years, subtracting resources from students who require additional support to counterbalance not only the learning losses experienced, but also the socio-psychological effects of the pandemic. Funding will also be needed to ensure that the pandemic's impact does not fall disproportionately on the poorest and most vulnerable students (World Bank Group, 2020[78]). In 2020, the World Bank estimated that in some countries, particularly high-income ones, education spending in 2021 was forecast to decline in real terms along with overall government spending: they estimated a projected decrease of 2.6% in the real growth of education spending per capita (World Bank Group, 2020[78]). After the 2008 financial crisis, OECD countries showed that education budgets were initially protected, but in 2010 a third of countries cut their overall education budgets while just under a half of countries cut teacher salaries (OECD, 2013[79]).

In all countries, the pandemic has placed a spotlight on the need to use resources as efficiently and equitably as possible. Equity and inclusion issues should be analysed with particular care in the aftermath of this crisis. As the gaps increase, due to the difficulties of the pandemic, countries may find it difficult to support their most vulnerable students in times of economic and social turmoil. Research should provide inputs on how efficiently to address issues of equity and inclusion, and present countries and policy makers with enough evidence to support targeted policies.

Teachers play a fundamental role in this by designing and implementing inclusive teaching practices that adequately meet diverse student needs and learning styles. To do so, teachers must have the knowledge, skills and tools to incorporate inclusive teaching strategies into pedagogies, curricula and assessments while promoting an inclusive classroom environment. Education systems need to ensure that teachers are adequately prepared for inclusive teaching and supported throughout their career.

Data from TALIS 2018 show that, on average across OECD countries, at least one in five teachers (22%) reports the need for training on special education needs, while one in three teachers (32%) in lower secondary education reports a shortage of teachers able to teach students with SEN. Having teachers capable of adequately responding to the needs of students with SEN is also among the most common resource issues highlighted in TALIS 2018. Furthermore, TALIS 2018 shows that, on average, one in three teachers (33%) does not feel sufficiently equipped to meet the challenges of teaching in multicultural settings. Training on multicultural/multilingual settings is reported as the second-highest need for professional learning recognised by 15% of teachers (see Figure 2.7). This becomes increasingly critical when acknowledging that, on average across OECD countries, 17% to 30% of teachers work in schools with a culturally or linguistically diverse student population. Furthermore, only around three-fifths of teachers in multicultural schools (62%) work in settings supporting activities or organisations that promote students' expression of diverse ethnic and cultural identities (OECD, 2019[80]). Also, the share of teachers reporting a high need for training on special education needs and participating in professional learning on special education needs has risen in the last five years across many OECD countries.

The ways teachers are prepared to teach in diverse classrooms, both through initial teacher education and professional learning, can have considerable impact on student well-being, academically, socio-emotionally and psychologically. These interventions relate to equipping prospective and practising teachers with core competences for inclusive teaching (such as critical reflection, uncovering hidden bias, global competence and growth mindset) to develop inclusive curricula, pedagogies and assessments. Other inclusive teaching interventions target students more directly, such as instructing them about the threat and effects of stereotypes, and promoting positive values and a growth mindset approach to foster diversity and inclusion among classmates. To promote inclusive and diverse classroom environments, the inclusion of more diverse teachers also plays an important role, with effects on student academic outcomes, engagement and socio-emotional well-being.

Figure 2.7 **Needs for training on diversity and inclusion (TALIS 2018)**

Percentage of lower secondary teachers and principals reporting the following (OECD average-31)

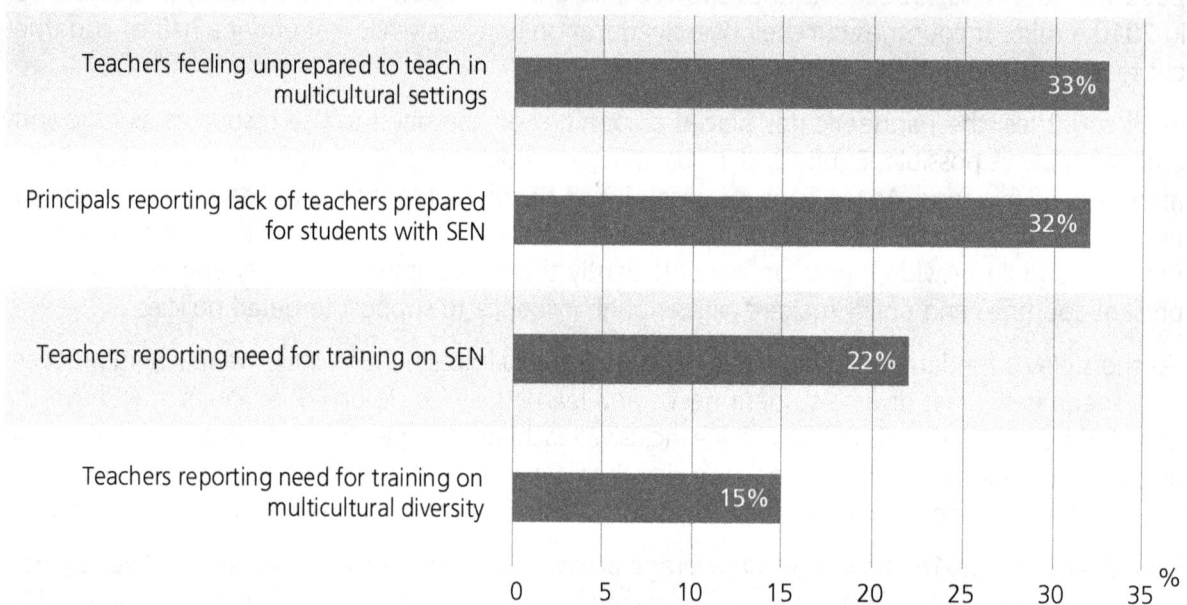

Source: Averages based on OECD countries included in TALIS 2018: Alberta (Canada), Australia, Austria, Belgium (and Flemish Community), Chile, Colombia, Czech Republic, Denmark, England (UK), Estonia, Finland, France, Hungary, Iceland, Israel, Italy, Japan, Korea, Latvia, Lithuania, Mexico, Netherlands, New Zealand, Norway, Portugal, Slovak Republic, Slovenia, Spain, Sweden, Turkey, United States.
Source: OECD (2019[80]), *TALIS 2018 Results (Volume I): Teachers and School Leaders as Lifelong Learners,* https://doi.org/10.1787/1d0bc92a-en.

What teachers teach (curriculum), how they teach (pedagogy) and how they monitor student learning (assessment) contribute to promoting or hampering diversity and inclusion in the classroom. Similarly, through the ways they critically think and reflect, perceive themselves and others, and uncover their unconscious biases, teachers can develop learning spaces where diversity is valued and inclusion is promoted. Managing an inclusive classroom environment by modelling an inclusive language, disarming micro-aggressions and promoting inclusive seating or virtual classroom arrangements, is also key for inclusive teaching. PISA 2018 asked students about their perception of their teachers' attitudes towards people from other cultural groups, and where students perceived their teachers to be discriminating, they tended to report more discriminative attitudes themselves.

In short, teachers play a fundamental role in promoting inclusive learning environments for all students. Of the factors that are most susceptible to policy change, those related to teachers and teaching have the greatest influence over student learning.

NOTES

1. Gross domestic product (GDP) is the standard measure of the value added created through the production of goods and services in a country during a certain period. Source: https://data.oecd.org/gdp/gross-domestic-product-gdp.htm.

2. Even though the United States generally adopt the term "race", the Strength through Diversity Project prefers the term "ethnicity" due to sensitivity of various OECD countries towards the former term.

REFERENCES

Abt Associates (2016), *A Summary of the Evidence on Inclusive Education*, https://www.abtassociates.com/insights/publications/report/summary-of-the-evidence-on-inclusive-education#:~:text=After%20reviewing%20evidence%20from%20more (accessed on 13 January 2021). [23]

Allport, G. (1954), *The nature of prejudice,* Addison-Welsey Publishing. [25]

Amor, A. et al. (2018), "International perspectives and trends in research on inclusive education: a systematic review", *International Journal of Inclusive Education*, Vol. 23/12, pp. 1277-1295, https://doi.org/10.1080/13603116.2018.1445304. [3]

AuCoin, A., G. Porter and K. Baker-Korotkov (2020), "New Brunswick's journey to inclusive education", *PROSPECTS*, Vol. 49/3-4, pp. 313-328, https://doi.org/10.1007/s11125-020-09508-8. [30]

Biederman, J. and S. Faraone (2006), "The Effects of Attention-Deficit/Hyperactivity Disorder on Employment and Household Income", *Medscape General Medicine,* Vol. 8/3. [14]

Brown, C. (2015), *The Educational, Psychological and Social Impact of Discrimination on the Immigrant Child,* Migration Policy Institute, https://www.migrationpolicy.org/research/educational-psychological-and-social-impact-discrimination-immigrant-child. [44]

Brussino, O. (2021), "Building capacity for inclusive teaching: Policies and practices to prepare all teachers for diversity and inclusion", *OECD Education Working Papers*, No. 256, OECD Publishing, Paris, https://dx.doi.org/10.1787/57fe6a38-en. [76]

Brussino, O. (2020), "Mapping policy approaches and practices for the inclusion of students with special education needs", *OECD Education Working Papers*, No. 227, OECD Publishing, Paris, https://dx.doi.org/10.1787/600fbad5-en. [9]

Cerna, L. (2019), "Refugee education: Integration models and practices in OECD countries", *OECD Education Working Papers,* No. 203, OECD Publishing, Paris, https://dx.doi.org/10.1787/a3251a00-en. [49]

Commonwealth of Australia (2018), *Closing the Gap Prime Minister's Report 2018*, https://www.pmc.gov.au/sites/default/files/reports/closing-the-gap-2018/sites/default/files/ctg-report-20183872.pdf?a=1 (accessed on 15 September 2020). [54]

Dean, J. (2018), "Segregation effects on Australian Indigenous primary school achievement", *Asia Pacific Journal of Education*, pp. 1-17, https://doi.org/10.1080/02188791.2018.1509057. [21]

Diamond, G. and S. Winfield (2018), *Gender and inclusive education: the weak link in girls' education programming*, https://medium.com/ungei-blog/gender-and-inclusive-education-the-weak-link-in-girls-education-programming-2f5b0a2faf0f. [67]

Dowdall, C. and N. Colangelo (1982), "Underachieving Gifted Students: Review and Implications", *Gifted Child Quarterly,* Vol. 26/4, pp. 179-184, https://doi.org/10.1177/001698628202600406. [36]

European Agency for Special Needs and Inclusive Education (2018), *Evidence of the Link Between Inclusive Education and Social Inclusion: A Review of the Literature.* [33]

European Agency for Special Needs and Inclusive Education (2018), *Financing Policies for Inclusive Education Systems: Final Summary Report.* [12]

European Union Agency for Fundamental Rights (2020), *A long way to go for LGBTI equality,* https://fra.europa.eu/sites/default/files/fra_uploads/fra-2020-lgbti-equality-1_en.pdf (accessed on 22 February 2021). [69]

European Union Agency for Fundamental Rights (2017), *Second European Union Minorities and Discrimination Survey - Main Results*, Publications Office of the European Union, https://doi.org/10.2811/902610. [50]

European Union Agency for Fundamental Rights (2016), "EU-MIDIS II Second European Union Minorities and Discrimination Survey Roma-Selected findings", https://doi.org/10.2811/189587. [51]

Ferrant, G. and A. Kolev (2016), *The economic cost of gender-based discrimination in social institutions*, https://www.oecd.org/dev/development-gender/SIGI_cost_final.pdf. [16]

Fryer, R. and S. Levitt (2010), "An Empirical Analysis of the Gender Gap in Mathematics", *American Economic Association*, pp. 210-240. [28]

Guiso, L. et al. (2008), "Culture, Gender, and Math", *Science*, Vol. 320/5880, pp. 1164-1165. [27]

Halpern, D. et al. (2011), "The Pseudoscience of Single-Sex Schooling", *Science*, Vol. 333/6050, pp. 1706-1707, https://doi.org/10.1126/science.1205031. [26]

Hanushek, E. and L. Woessmann (2020), "The economic impacts of learning losses", *OECD Education Working Papers*, No. 225, OECD Publishing, Paris, https://dx.doi.org/10.1787/21908d74-en. [6]

Hanushek, E. and L. Woessmann (2007), *The Role Of Education Quality For Economic Growth*, The World Bank, https://doi.org/10.1596/1813-9450-4122. [5]

Heuser, B., K. Wang and S. Shahid (2017), "Global Dimensions of Gifted and Talented Education: The Influence of National Perceptions on Policies and Practices", *Global Education Review*, Vol. 4/1, pp. 4-21, https://eric.ed.gov/?id=EJ1137994. [38]

Human Rights Campaign (2013), *Growing Up LGBT in America: HRC Youth Survey Report Key Findings*. [68]

Juvonen, J., K. Kogachi and S. Graham (2017), "When and How Do Students Benefit From Ethnic Diversity in Middle School?", *Child Development*, Vol. 89/4, pp. 1268-1282, https://doi.org/10.1111/cdev.12834. [59]

Juvonen, J., A. Nishina and S. Graham (2006), "Ethnic Diversity and Perceptions of Safety in Urban Middle Schools", *Psychological Science*, Vol. 17/5, pp. 393-400, https://doi.org/10.1111/j.1467-9280.2006.01718.x. [58]

Kao, G. and J. Thompson (2003), "Racial and Ethnic Stratification in Educational Achievement and Attainment", *Annual Reviews*, pp. 417-442. [18]

Koehler, D. et al. (2017), *Discrimination against sexual minorities in education and housing: evidence from two field experiments in Serbia*, http://documents.worldbank.org/curated/en/161011522071811826/Discrimination-against-sexual-minorities-in-education-and-housing-evidence-from-two-field-experiments-in-Serbia. [71]

Kosciw, J. et al. (2020), *The 2019 National School Climate Survey: The Experiences of Lesbian, Gay, Bisexual, Transgender, and Queer Youth in Our Nation's Schools*, GLSEN, https://www.glsen.org/sites/default/files/2020-11/NSCS19-111820.pdf (accessed on 22 February 2021). [74]

Kosciw, J. et al. (2010), *The 2009 National School Climate Survey: The Experiences of Lesbian, Gay, Bisexual, Transgender, and Queer Youth in Our Nation's Schools*, https://files.eric.ed.gov/fulltext/ED512338.pdf. [73]

Kosciw, J. et al. (2012), "The Effect of Negative School Climate on Academic Outcomes for LGBT Youth and the Role of In-School Supports", *Journal of School Violence*, Vol. 12/1, pp. 45-63, https://doi.org/10.1080/15388220.2012.732546. [72]

McArdle, N. and D. Acevedo-Garcia (2017), *Consequences of Segregation for Children's Opportunity and Wellbeing*, President and Fellows of Harvard College. [19]

Mezzanotte, C. (2022), "The social and economic rationale of inclusive education: An overview of the outcomes in education for diverse groups of students", *OECD Education Working Papers*, No. 263, OECD Publishing, Paris, https://dx.doi.org/10.1787/bff7a85d-en. [75]

Mezzanotte, C. (2020), "Policy approaches and practices for the inclusion of students with attention-deficit hyperactivity disorder (ADHD)", *OECD Education Working Papers*, No. 238, OECD Publishing, Paris, https://dx.doi.org/10.1787/49af95e0-en. [11]

Morgon Banks, L. and S. Polack (2015), *The Economic Costs of Exclusion and Gains of Inclusion of People with Disabilities: Evidence from Low and Middle Income Countries*, https://www.iapb.org/wp-content/uploads/CBM_Costs-of-Exclusion-and-Gains-of-Inclusion-Report_2015.pdf (accessed on 12 February 2021). [34]

New Brunswick Department of Education and Early Childhood Development (2019), *Summary statistics: School year 2018-2019*, https://bit.ly/3iNnJBh (accessed on 21 September 2020). [31]

New Brunswick Health Council (2019), *New Brunswick 2018-2019 student wellness survey — Grades 6-12*, https://nbhc.ca/all-publications/nbsws-grades-6-12-2018-2019 (accessed on 21 September 2020). [29]

Nishina, A. et al. (2019), "Ethnic Diversity and Inclusive School Environments", *Educational Psychologist*, Vol. 54/4, pp. 306-321, https://doi.org/10.1080/00461520.2019.1633923. [24]

OECD (forthcoming), *The Future of Teachers and Teaching*. [81]

OECD (2020), *All Hands In? Making Diversity Work for All*, OECD Publishing, Paris, https://dx.doi.org/10.1787/efb14583-en. [62]

OECD (2020), *Education GPS Gender*, https://gpseducation.oecd.org/revieweducationpolicies/#!node=41753&filter=all. [64]

OECD (2020), *Over the Rainbow? The Road to LGBTI Inclusion*, OECD Publishing, Paris, https://dx.doi.org/10.1787/8d2fd1a8-en. [70]

OECD (2020), *PISA 2018 Results (Volume VI): Are Students Ready to Thrive in an Interconnected World?*, PISA, OECD Publishing, Paris, https://dx.doi.org/10.1787/d5f68679-en. [46]

OECD (2020), *The impact of COVID-19 on student equity and inclusion: supporting vulnerable students during school closures and school re-openings*, https://www.oecd.org/coronavirus/policy-responses/the-impact-of-covid-19-on-student-equity-and-inclusion-supporting-vulnerable-students-during-school-closures-and-school-re-openings-d593b5c8/ (accessed on 1 April 2022). [77]

OECD (2019), *OECD Economic Surveys: Slovak Republic 2019*, OECD Publishing, Paris, https://dx.doi.org/10.1787/eco_surveys-svk-2019-en. [20]

OECD (2019), *PISA 2018 Results (Volume II): Where All Students Can Succeed*, PISA, OECD Publishing, Paris, https://dx.doi.org/10.1787/b5fd1b8f-en. [17]

OECD (2019), *TALIS 2018 Results (Volume I): Teachers and School Leaders as Lifelong Learners*, TALIS, OECD Publishing, Paris, https://dx.doi.org/10.1787/1d0bc92a-en. [80]

OECD (2018), *Indigenous Employment and Skills Strategies in Canada*, OECD Reviews on Local Job Creation, OECD Publishing, Paris, https://dx.doi.org/10.1787/9789264300477-en. [57]

OECD (2018), *PISA 2018 Database*, http://www.oecd.org/pisa/data/2018database/ (accessed on 13 February 2020). [43]

OECD (2018), *The Resilience of Students with an Immigrant Background: Factors that Shape Well-being*, OECD Reviews of Migrant Education, OECD Publishing, Paris, https://dx.doi.org/10.1787/9789264292093-en. [42]

OECD (2017), *Promising Practices in Supporting Success for Indigenous Students*, OECD Publishing, Paris, https://dx.doi.org/10.1787/9789264279421-en. [52]

OECD (2015), T*he ABC of Gender Equality in Education: Aptitude, Behaviour, Confidence*, PISA, OECD Publishing, Paris, https://dx.doi.org/10.1787/9789264229945-en. [65]

OECD (2013), "What is the Impact of the Economic Crisis on Public Education Spending?", *Education Indicators in Focus*, No. 18, OECD Publishing, Paris, https://dx.doi.org/10.1787/5jzbb2sprz20-en. [79]

OECD (2012), *Closing the Gender Gap: Act Now*, OECD Publishing, Paris, https://dx.doi.org/10.1787/9789264179370-en. [66]

OECD (2012), *Equity and Quality in Education: Supporting Disadvantaged Students and Schools*, OECD Publishing, Paris, https://dx.doi.org/10.1787/9789264130852-en. [4]

OECD (2010), *The High Cost of Low Educational Performance: The Long-run Economic Impact of Improving PISA Outcomes*, PISA, OECD Publishing, Paris, https://dx.doi.org/10.1787/9789264077485-en. [13]

OECD (2006), "The Returns to Education: Links between Education, Economic Growth and Social Outcomes", in *Education at a Glance 2006: OECD Indicators*, OECD Publishing, Paris, https://dx.doi.org/10.1787/eag-2006-11-en. [7]

Pettigrew, T. and L. Tropp (2006), "A meta-analytic test of intergroup contact theory.", *Journal of Personality and Social Psychology*, Vol. 90/5, pp. 751-783, https://doi.org/10.1037/0022-3514.90.5.751. [45]

Ritchotte, J., M. Matthews and C. Flowers (2014), "The Validity of the Achievement-Orientation Model for Gifted Middle School Students", *Gifted Child Quarterly*, Vol. 58/3, pp. 183-198, https://doi.org/10.1177/0016986214534890. [37]

Ruijs, N. and T. Peetsma (2009), "Effects of inclusion on students with and without special educational needs reviewed", **Educational Research Review**, Vol. 4/2, pp. 67-79, https://doi.org/10.1016/j.edurev.2009.02.002. [22]

Rutigliano, A. (2020), "Inclusion of Roma students in Europe: A literature review and examples of policy initiatives", *OECD Education Working Papers*, No. 228, OECD Publishing, Paris, https://dx.doi.org/10.1787/8ce7d6eb-en. [10]

Senate Employment Workplace Relations, Small Business and Education References Committee (2001), *The education of gifted children*, Parliament House, https://www.aph.gov.au/Parliamentary_Business/Committees/Senate/Education_Employment_and_Workplace_Relations/Completed_inquiries/1999-02/gifted/report/contents (accessed on 25 January 2021). [39]

Stats New Zealand (2020), *Education outcomes improving for Māori and Pacific peoples*, https://www.stats.govt.nz/news/education-outcomes-improving-for-maori-and-pacific-peoples (accessed on 9 September 2020). [55]

Stolle, D., S. Soroka and R. Johnston (2008), "When Does Diversity Erode Trust? Neighborhood Diversity, Interpersonal Trust and the Mediating Effect of Social Interactions", *Political Studies*, Vol. 56/1, pp. 57-75, https://doi.org/10.1111/j.1467-9248.2007.00717.x. [61]

Toulouse, P. (2016), *What Matters in Indigenous Education: Implementing a Vision Committed to Holism, Diversity and Engagement,* People for Education, https://peopleforeducation.ca/wp-content/uploads/2017/07/MWM-What-Matters-in-Indigenous-Education.pdf (accessed on 21 February 2020). [56]

Tropp, L. and S. Saxena (2018), *Re-Weaving the Social Fabric through Integrated Schools: How Intergroup Contact Prepares Youth to Thrive in a Multiracial Society.* [60]

U46 (2020), *Gifted Services for Students in Grades 4-6,* https://www.u-46.org/Page/8998 (accessed on 21 February 2021). [40]

UNESCO (2020), *Global Education Monitoring Report 2020,* UNESCO. [8]

UNESCO (2009), *Towards Inclusive Education for Children with Disabilities: A Guideline,* https://unesdoc.unesco.org/ark:/48223/pf0000192480. [1]

UNHCR (2017), *Left Behind: Refugee Education in Crisis,* https://www.unhcr.org/59b696f44.pdf (accessed on 10 June 2021). [47]

UNICEF (2020), *Girls' education,* https://www.unicef.org/education/girls-education#:~:text=Worldwide%2C%20132%20million%20girls%20are,The%20reasons%20are%20many (accessed on 12 September 2020). [63]

UNICEF (2018), *"Refugee and migrant crisis in Europe" Humanitarian Situation Report # 29,* https://www.unicef.org/media/104191/file/Refugee%20and%20Migrant%20Crisis%20in%20Europe%20Humanitarian%20Situation%20Report%20No.40,%2030%20June%202021.pdf (accessed on 1 April 2022). [48]

UNICEF (2016), *Uprooted - the growing crisis for refugee and migrant children,* https://data.unicef.org/resources/uprooted-growing-crisis-refugee-migrant-children/ (accessed on 1 April 2022). [41]

UNICEF (2014), *Conceptualizing Inclusive Education and Contextualizing it within the UNICEF Mission,* https://www.unicef.org/eca/sites/unicef.org.eca/files/IE_Webinar_Booklet_1_0.pdf (accessed on 12 June 2020). [2]

Wannell, T. and S. Currie (2016), *Determinants of Participation in Indigenous Labour Market Programs: Final Report,* Social Research and Demonstration Corporation for Aboriginal Affairs Directorate Employment and Social Development Canada, http://www.srdc.org/media/199959/ilmp-determinants-report.pdf (accessed on 9 September 2020). [53]

Washington Group on Disability Statistics (2018), *Selected SDG Indicators Disaggregated by Disability Status,* https://www.washingtongroup-disability.com/fileadmin/uploads/wg/Documents/Disagregation-Data-Report_.pdf (accessed on 15 February 2020). [32]

World Bank Group (2020), *The impact of the COVID-19 pandemic on education financing,* http://pubdocs.worldbank.org/en/734541589314089887/Covid-and-Ed-Finance-final.pdf (accessed on 28 January 2021). [78]

World Bank Group (2010), *Roma inclusion : An economic opportunity for Bulgaria, Czech Republic, Romania and Serbia* (English). [15]

Yarrison, B. (2018), *"If not us, then who? If not now, then when?", Journal of the National Collegiate Honors Council,* Vol. 19/2, https://digitalcommons.unl.edu/nchcjournal/581. [35]